HISTORIA
DO
PREDESTINADO
PEREGRINO,
E SEU IRMAÕ PRECITO.

Em a qual debayxo de huma mysteriosa
Parabola se descreve o sucesso feliz
do que se hade salvar, & a infeliz
sorte do que se hade
condenar,

DEDICADA
AÔ PEREGRINO CELESTIAL,
S. FRANCISCO XAVIER,
Apostolo do Oriente.

COMPOSTA.
PELO P. ALEXANDRE DE GUSMAM
da Companhia de JESU da Provincia
do Brasil.

※

LISBOA ORIENTAL.
Na Officina de FELIPPE DE SOUSA VILLELA.

A custa de Domingos Gonçalves, mercador
de Livros. Anno de 1728.

Com todas as Licenças necessarias.

Title page of the 1728 Portuguese edition.

The Story of the Predestined Pilgrim and His Brother Reprobate

MEDIEVAL AND RENAISSANCE
TEXTS AND STUDIES

VOLUME 489

MEDIEVAL AND RENAISSANCE
LATIN AMERICA

VOLUME 2

The Story of the Predestined Pilgrim and His Brother Reprobate

In which, through a mysterious parable, is told the felicitous success of the one saved and the unfortunate lot of the one condemned.

Dedicated to the Celestial Pilgrim
Saint Francis Xavier,
Apostle of the Orient

Composed by
Father Alexandre de Gusmão
of the Company of JESUS
in the Province of Brazil.

EVORA
With all the necessary licenses
at the University Press
1682

Translated, with an introduction and index
by
Christopher C. Lund

ARIZONA CENTER FOR MEDIEVAL

ACMRS

AND RENAISSANCE STUDIES

Tempe, Arizona
2016

THE ARIZONA CENTER FOR
MEDIEVAL &
RENAISSANCE
STUDIES

Published by ACMRS (Arizona Center for Medieval and Renaissance Studies)
Tempe, Arizona
© 2016 Arizona Board of Regents for Arizona State University.
All Rights Reserved.

Library of Congress Cataloging-in-Publication Data

Names: Gusmão, Alexandre de, 1629-1724, author. | Lund, Christopher C.,
    translator.
Title: The story of the Predestined Pilgrim and his brother reprobate : in which,
    through a mysterious parable, is told the felicitous success of the one saved
    and the unfortunate lot of the one condemned. / composed by Father
    Alexandre de Gusmão of the company of Jesus in the province of Brazil ;
    translated, with an introduction and index by Christopher C. Lund.
Other titles: História do Predestinado Peregrino e seu irmao precito. English
Description: Tempe, Arizona : Arizona Center for Medieval and Renaissance
    Studies, 2016. | Series: Medieval and Renaissance texts and studies ; 489 |
    Includes bibliographical references and index.
Identifiers: LCCN 2016040812 | ISBN 9780866985444 (hardcover : acid-free
    paper)
Subjects: LCSH: Portuguese fiction--Classical period, 1500-1700. | Allegories.
Classification: LCC PQ9231.G87 H5713 2016 | DDC 869.3--dc23
LC record available at https://lccn.loc.gov/2016040812

∞
This book is made to last. It is set in Adobe Caslon Pro,
smyth-sewn and printed on acid-free paper to library specifications.
Printed in the United States of America

This book is dedicated to the memory of
Father Alexandre de Gusmão, S.J.,
and to lovers of religious allegory.

TABLE OF CONTENTS

ACKNOWLEDGMENTS

This project has been a labor of love. Love's labor may have dwindled or been lost, however, without the support of the Department of Spanish and Portuguese and the College of Humanities at Brigham Young University, which gave me encouragement and, occasionally, blocks of free time to sort out textual challenges. I was warmly welcomed by the Knights of Columbus Vatican Film Library of Saint Louis University and by the Portuguese Biblioteca Nacional in Lisbon; thank you for your exquisite collections.

I am grateful for grants from the Portuguese National Archive (Torre do Tombo) and the John Carter Brown Library. Access to their rich holdings helped me successfully to negotiate a number of perplexities.

A special note of thanks to Laura Rawlins for her fine and timely editing.

INTRODUCTION

The Story of Predestined Pilgrim and His Brother Reprobate is the first English translation of the 1682 allegorical novel of salvation,[1] *A história do Predestinado Peregrino e seu irmão Precito*, written in Brazil by the Jesuit priest Father Alexandre de Gusmão (1629–1724), and published in Portugal.[2] Two more Portuguese editions followed in 1685 and in 1728.[3] Two distinct Spanish translations, done by anonymous Jesuits, appeared in 1696 and in 1815, the first in Barcelona, and the second in Mexico City on the occasion of the Spanish reinstatement of the Jesuit order there. This book is a pedagogical complement to the academic initiatives of the Jesuit order, spelled out in the *Ratio atque Institutio Studiorum Societatis Iesu* (1599), and was warmly embraced by the members of this order. But it saw only these five editions, perhaps because its fate was closely tied to the order that produced it: the Jesuits and all things Jesuit were abruptly expelled from Brazil in 1759 and from the Spanish Empire nine years later, in 1768.

---

[1] The publisher of Gusmão's first edition was Miguel Deslandes. Active for some thirty-five years until his death in 1704, he published at least ten other titles in 1682. They included legal tractates, a Portuguese translation of Tasso's *La Gerusalemme liberata*, a genealogy of the House of Savoy, and the long-awaited second volume of sermons by Father Antonio Vieira (1608–1697), Gusmão's coreligionary in Brazil.

[2] Unlike other Latin American colonies in which printing occurred in the sixteenth century (e.g., Mexico in 1539 and Peru in 1581), printing presses would not arrive in Brazil until 1808, when King D. João VI moved his court to Rio de Janeiro, fleeing the Napoleonic invasion of the Iberian Peninsula. All manuscripts produced in pre-1808 Brazil had to pass censorship in the motherland, where they were usually also subsequently published.

[3] See Cesar Augusto Martins Miranda de Freitas, "Alexandre de Gusmão: Da Literatura Jesuíta de Intervenção Social" (doctoral dissertation, Faculdade de Letras da Universidade do Porto, 2011). To date, this is the best study of Alexandre de Gusmão and his sources. Freitas unfortunately repeats the error begun by Diogo Barbosa Machado (*Biblioteca Lusitana*. Lisbon, 1741), that the third edition of Gusmão's allegory was published in 1724. Innocêncio had called the 1724 edition into question, having never seen a copy of that text. The printing information in my personal copy of the last Portuguese edition is as follows: *Lisboa Oriental. Na Officina de Felippe de Sousa Villela. À custa de Domingos Gonçalves, mercador de Livros. Anno de 1728.* Thus, Barbosa Machado's mention of the so-called 1724 edition is wrong on two counts: he read *Villa* for *Villela*, and 1724 for 1728.

Allegory has long been a favorite literary device in both prose and poetry. The Bible is suffused with allegory. Augustine of Hippo employed it in *Civitate Dei* (fifth century). It is prominent in Raymond Llull's *Blanquerna* (ca. 1283). Dante drew deeply from the wellspring of allegory for his *Divine Comedy* (1309–1320). Allegory is characteristically present in most medieval classics,[4] and it is certainly a common apparatus in sixteenth- and seventeenth-century Western literature. It is fair to say that the English allegorical tradition culminates with the writings of John Bunyan (1628–1688), whose masterpiece *Pilgrim's Progress* has never been out of print since its publication in 1678. Why mention Bunyan in an introduction to the work of a Jesuit? Even as the Protestant Bunyan was writing *Pilgrim's Progress* in his cell in the Bedford County Gaol, five thousand miles away in Brazil, in the tiny village of Belém da Cachoeira, Father Alexandre de Gusmão, S.J.—Bunyan's junior by a year—was writing his first book, *A Escola de Belém: Jesus nascido no prescpio* (The School of Bethlehem: Jesus born in a stable), a 300-page quarto that explores the principal Christic metaphors through an allegorical reading of the life of Jesus as contained in the gospels.[5] Bunyan's *Pilgrim's Progress* and Gusmão's *Predestined Pilgrim* (1682) may be seen as the two Christian bookends of seventeenth-century Western prose that take as their theme man's earthly sojourn in search of the New Jerusalem. Were these two authors aware of each other? It seems doubtful, but it remains within the realm of speculation. Although Jesuit presence was sporadic in England, anti-Catholic sentiment had waxed strongest precisely during the years 1678 and 1681, and Jesuit suffering in England would become notorious.[6] Was Gusmão's *Predestined Pilgrim* written as a Roman Catholic response to Bunyan's *Pilgrim's Progress*, then in its eighth edition? Possibly, but probably not. Spurred by the mandates of the *Ratio Studiorum* and his devotion to the prospect of educating Portuguese colonial youth, Gusmão had been developing his own agenda that, retrospectively, can be seen as having fortuitously synchronized with that of Bunyan.[7]

---

[4] See, for example, G. R. Boys-Stones, ed., *Metaphor, Allegory, and the Classical Tradition: Ancient Thought and Modern Revisions* (Oxford: Oxford University Press, 2003), or J. Stephen Russell, ed., *Allegoresis: The Craft of Allegory in Medieval Literature* (New York: Garland, 1988).

[5] Evora: Officina da Academia, 1678. This treatise, a kind of precursor to the more structured narrative of the *Predestined Pilgrim*, analyzes the particulars of the life of Jesus as elements of a salvific pedagogy. It is the first pedagogy written in Brazil.

[6] See John P. Kenyon, *The Popish Plot* (New Haven, CT: Phoenix Press, 2001). During the period 1678–1681, nine Jesuits were executed and twelve died in prison.

[7] Besides establishing, in 1686, the first boarding school in Brazil, called the Provincial Seminary of Bethlehem, Gusmão published the following works: *Menino Cristão* [The Christian Young Man] (Lisbon: Miguel Deslandes, Impressor del Rei, 1695); *Arte de criar bem os filhos* [The Art of Raising Children] (Lisbon: Miguel Deslandes, 1685); *Meditações para todos os dias da semana* [Meditations for Every Day of the Week] (Lisbon: Miguel Deslandes, 1689); *Maria Rosa de Nazaret nas montanhas de Hebron* [Mary, Rose

To date, however, only Bunyan's Pilgrim has captured our imagination.[8] Bunyan, the Protestant, writing from the jail to which he was sentenced for preaching the gospel in the fields of Bedford, England, without a permit, engages his reader with the tale of his protagonist, Christian, who sets out in search of his own salvation, so compelled to begin his urgent quest that he abandons wife and family to do so. Gusmão, the Roman Catholic Jesuit, penned his allegory in the hinterland village of Belém da Cachoeira, Bahia, some seventy kilometers west of Salvador da Bahia, the then-capital of Brazil. Predictably less angstful than the Bunyan's Protestant Christian, the Predestined Pilgrim is lead carefully and surely to the New Jerusalem — *with* his wife and family, and with the benefit of guided, programmed Roman Catholic intervention, while his brother Reprobate and family, who set out together with Predestined, follow a divergent path

---

of Nazareth in the Mountains of Hebron] (Lisbon: Officina Real Deslandesiana, 1715); *Eleição entre o bem e o mal eterno* [Choosing Between Eternal Good or Evil] (Lisbon: Officina da Musica, 1720); *O corvo e a pomba na Arca de Noé no sentido alegórico e moral* [The Raven and the Dove on Noah's Ark in the Allegorico-Moral Sense] (Lisbon: Bernardo da Costa, Impressor da Religião de Malta, 1734); *Árvore da vida Jesus crucificado* [The Tree of Life: Jesus Crucified] (Lisbon: Bernardo da Costa, Impressor da Religião de Malta, 1734).

  [8] When Bunyan's allegory was translated into Portuguese and published in 1782 in Lisbon on the press of Francisco Rolland, Gusmão's work was long forgotten. The title page of this translation of Bunyan claims that permission to publish the work had been granted by the Real Mesa Censoria (Royal Board of Censorship), a task force that scrutinized questions of orthodoxy, but no licenses are printed in the book. Nor is Bunyan's authorship recognized. The translator's preface reads: "When I found this novel titled *Pilgrimage of a Christian*, in the allegory of a dream, I became determined to translate it so that our nation might have a book whose original, being English, is found today translated into a number of languages. Everyone knows how the same truths move the souls of men, whether in fictions, emblems, or parables; for delighting in the reading, the reader is taught without scandal. The very wise and omnipotent founder of Christianity inspires us through the lessons of celestial doctrine that He teaches us; He reprehends and warns the people through parables and allegories. The classical writers of antiquity used the same system. [. . .] Man recognizes in this allegorical fiction that the world deceives him and that its ideas draw him towards it. But the true and enlightened Christian abandons that which can seduce him, preferring a rational path that illuminates his spirit, grounded in the eternal truths of sound doctrine that Christ and his apostles taught. The sincere characters in this morality play spring forth in such a lively and edifying way that they not only delight, but also convince and oblige the reader. Can such a book be anything but useful?" A similar translation of *Pilgrim's Progress* had appeared in Madrid six years earlier: *La peregrinación de un christiano, o Viage a la ciudad celeste, escrito en la alegoria de un sueño* [The Pilgrimage of a Christian, or Journey to the Celestial City, Written in the Allegory of a Dream], trad. del Frances al Castellano por Don Felix Galisteo [. . .]. (Madrid: En la Imprenta de Pedro Marín, 1776).

to Hell. Although perhaps generic equivalents, *Predestined Pilgrim* must not be compared to *Pilgrim's Progress* but rather *with* it.

The literary antecedent of all Christian souls' journeys through mortality is sketched out in chapter 11 of Paul's epistle to the Hebrews:

> 13 All these died according to faith, not having received the promises, but beholding them afar off, and saluting them, and confessing that *they are pilgrims and strangers on the earth.*

> 14 For they that say these things do signify that *they seek a country.*

> 15 And *truly if they had been mindful of that from whence they came out, they had doubtless time to return.*

> 16 But now *they desire a better, that is to say, a heavenly country. Therefore God is not ashamed to be called their God;* for *he hath prepared for them a city.*[9]

All subsequent pilgrimages, it may be said, draw from this source in one way or another. Both Gusmão and Bunyan refer directly or indirectly to this Pauline provenance, but there are, of course, many subtle differences in the two narratives.

Though they illustrate essentially the same quest—for they are both stories that follow "Every Christian's" advance through the vicissitudes of earthly plights to eventual salvation in the New Jerusalem—Bunyan's work is an existential piece, written from the perspective of the personal duress and the solitude of his own jail cell, about the earthy "cell" of Every Christian, each of whom must find salvation and be urgent about it. Gusmão's tale, on the other hand, extols the centuries-old ecclesiastical template of the Catholic Church and its clergy, whose sacraments and rites are proffered to every reader as a sure, if gradual, solution to life's challenges. Like his protagonist Christian, who feels compelled to run with his hands over his ears in search of salvation alone, abandoning his wife and children, Bunyan's decision to remain in the Bedford jail, alone, seems to have been a conscious act. Apparently he could have walked out at any time, rejoining a wife and family (whom he, too, had abandoned), with but a promise to authorities that he would not preach again without a license. This may be seen as his studied attempt to explore what we might call a pre-Kierkegaardian Christian angst—the same anxiety that motivates his Pilgrim to progress. Alone, on his own terms, without the distractions of family, neighbors, or other obligations, Bunyan can spin out the story of a pilgrim who, in turn, spins out his story of salvation. Our Jesuit priest, Gusmão, on the other hand—arguably from a "married" perspective, for to be vowed is to be married to Christ—does *not* have to abandon his family, the Church, to whom he has been called to minister. Inter-

---

[9] Douay-Rheims, 1899 American Edition; my emphasis.

estingly, the protagonists of his allegory, Predestined and Reprobate, both set out on their quests *with* their respective families: Predestined, married to Reason (without whom he undertakes nothing), and father of children, Good Desire and Upright Intention; Reprobate, married to Twisted Thinking (also without whom he does nothing) and father to their children, Bad Desire and Twisted Intention. In other words, for Gusmão and, by extension, for Roman Catholics, salvation is a family affair right from the start.

Pilgrim Zeitgeist

By the seventeenth century, pilgrimages to the Holy Land had become well institutionalized.[10] Nevertheless, physical, financial, and other reasons prevented most persons, despite religious inclinations to do a pilgrimage, from making the trek to the Holy Land or even to Santiago de Compostela in Galicia, Spain, the most popular pilgrimage site in medieval and Renaissance Europe. But all souls were free to consider their particular circumstance in life as their own valid pilgrimage.[11] Published guides, itineraries, or enchiridions, as such treatises were often called, could vicariously provide their readers the experience of a pilgrimage.

Textual traditions along these lines abounded in Europe. Guillaume de Deguileville, the French Cistercian who wrote *Le Pèlerinage de la Vie Humaine* (ca. 1330), was certainly a source for both Bunyan and Gusmão. Bunyan could have known *Pèlerinage* through John Wydgate's English translation,[12] while Gusmão may have seen any of the Castilian or Latin translations that appeared by the early sixteenth century. Gusmão, we remember, was a recipient of the allegorical tradition through the founders of his religious order, Ignatius Loyola and Francisco Xavier. He most probably knew also the *Espill de la vida religiosa*, written

---

[10] See Jonathan Sumption, *Pilgrimage* (London: Faber and Faber, 1975), for a thorough study of the motives and logistics of the medieval pilgrimage. The pilgrimage "was practiced in one form or another from late antiquity to the Reformation, and has maintained a fitful existence ever since [. . .] Writing in the 1520s, Erasmus looked forward to the rapid demise of the pilgrimage to Santiago. Yet the great Galician sanctuary was probably more prosperous in the seventeenth century than it had ever been in the middle ages" (302). See also Donald R. Howard, *Writers and Pilgrims: Medieval Pilgrimage Narratives and Their Posterity* (Berkeley: University of California Press, 1980), and Maria de Lurdes Correia Fernandes, *Espelhos, cartas e guias. Casamento e espiritualidade na Península Ibérica 1450–1700* (Porto: Instituto de Cultura Portuguesa, 1995), but which mentions only Gusmão's *Arte de Crear Filhos*.

[11] In Portugal, for example, they could undertake such pretended travel by reading Pantaleão de Aveiro, *Itinerário da Terra Sancta e suas particularidades* (Lisbon, 1593)

[12] See especially James Blanton Wharey, *A Study of the Sources of Bunyan's Allegories: With Special Reference to Deguileville's Pilgrimage of Man* (New York: Gordian Press, 1968).

by Miquel Comalada, a monk in the Sant Jeroni monastery in Barcelona.[13] And
Portugal had an allegorical tradition of its own. Many of the plays of Gil Vicente
(ca. 1465–ca. 1536?), who wrote in both Portuguese and Spanish, are steeped in
allegory.[14] More proximate to the life of Alexandre de Gusmão is Tristão Barbosa de Carvalho, whose *Peregrinação Cristão* would certainly have been known
to him as a teenager in Lisbon.[15] Though rich metaphors and allegorical passages
characterize many of these prior works, none are so complete an allegory from
beginning to end as are the novels of Bunyan and Gusmão. Both writers are
scholars and enjoyers of the doctrine of the gospel of Christ that carries throughout the New Testament. Both were the recipients of the powerful sixteenth-cen-
tury movements of the Protestant Reformation and the post-Tridentine Counter-
Reformation. Bunyan was absorbed in the exciting realization of his own calling.
We are fortunate that he allowed his gospel vision to percolate through the lay-
ers of his fertile imagination to emerge in the form of his novel.[16] We are no less
fortunate that Gusmão was similarly led to create his own allegorical fiction that
synthesizes the centuries-old Roman Catholic mission of saving souls, particularly through his Jesuit lens.

---

[13] Barcelona: Joan Rosenbach, 1515, and a subsequent Spanish translation published in Lisbon in 1541. This work was translated into English as *Desiderius, a Most Godly, Religious, and Delectable Dialogue* (Imprinted at Roane [i.e., England]: [English Secret
Press], by the permission of superiors, Anno 1604). Of interest to the Gusmão legacy is
the fact that the first Spanish translation of *Predestined* was published also in Barcelona,
not far from the birthplace Ignatius Loyola. That Gusmão was well aware of the expectation of pilgrimage for Jesuits is suggested in the dedication in his novel: "To the Celestial
Pilgrim Saint Francis Xavier, Apostle of the Orient." Did *Desiderius* influence Gusmão?
Probably. But *Predestined* stands on its own and is very different from it predecessor.
There are passages of vaguely similar dialogue, but *Desiderius* lacks the detailed catechis-
tic structure of *Predestined Pilgrim*, and is not a quest for salvation in the New Jerusalem.

[14] See especially Vicente's *Auto da Alma* [Play of the Soul], an Everyman's journey
through life, accosted by diabolical adversaries, and saved through refuge in the Church.
Of note is his "Three Ships Trilogy": the ship to Hell, the ship to Purgatory, and the ship
to Glory, clearly reminiscent of Dante's *Comedia*.

[15] Lisbon: por Geraldo da Vinha, 1620. The work covers the "creation of angels;
the world; the life, passion, and death of the Redeemer, and of Our Lady the Virgin; the
predestination and signs of the predestined unto the triumphant and celestial city of Jerusalem."

[16] Interestingly, Robert McCrum places *The Pilgrim's Progress* first in his list of the
one hundred best novels (*The Observer*, Saturday, 21 September 2013).

The Jesuits in Brazil

The Portuguese were part of Ignatius Loyola's enduring initiative from its inception. Simão Rodrigues (1510–1579), one of the six visionary friends at the University of Paris who took vows of poverty and chastity at the church of Montmartre in 1534, established the Jesuits in Portugal. In 1549, nine years after Pope Paul III formally accepted the new order of the Society of Jesus and blessed its mission, Fathers Nobrega and Anchieta arrived in Brazil. By 1554, these two talented priests were instrumental in laying the foundations of the city of São Paulo. Conflicts inevitably arose between the religious and the secular pioneers of Brazil. The Jesuits' purpose was the conversion of indigenous inhabitants to Christianity and the maintenance of Roman Catholic orthodoxy through catechesis among the Portuguese exiles and homesteaders. At the same time, marauding explorer colonists, or *bandeirantes* as they were known, made frequent incursions into the Brazilian interior, not in search of the "gold" of souls converted, but of precious metals and stones. They made slaves of the indigenous inhabitants they encountered and killed those who resisted capture. Jesuit zeal for conversion and the establishment of utopian indigenous settlements, or reductions—the first

Fig. 1: The church that still stands in Belém da Cachoeira, Bahia—all that remains from the School of Bethlehem complex built by Alexandre de Gusmão, S.J., in the 1680s.

republics in the New World and now almost forgotten—spread their effort away from São Paulo, southwest into what is now Paraguay and, finally, north to Peru. Jesuits, however, would remain in the urban centers of Brazil to educate its colonists. Fourteen-year-old Alexandre de Gusmão embraced the promise and excitement of Portuguese colonial life in Brazil as his ship entered the harbor in Guanabara Bay, Rio de Janeiro, in 1644, and found a home in the bustling community of about five thousand inhabitants, more than half of whom were African and indigenous slaves.

Gusmão's Life

Although most sources for biographical information on the life of Alexandre de Gusmão have followed what Diogo Barbosa Machado recorded in his *Bibliotheca Lusitana* (1741–1759), I am gratefully following the careful research of Miranda de Freitas, who incorporated much new data from the "Compendiaria Narratio Vitae et Virtutum P. Alexandre Gusmani," held in the Jesuit archives in the Vatican (Archivum Romanum Societatis Iesu: ARSI), known for many years to exist, but which was only recently discovered in Rome, and which I was not able to find or see during my own visit there. The following synopsis traces the long life of the author of *The Predestined Pilgrim* and derives from Barbosa Machado, Miranda de Freitas, and the ten-volume work by Serafim Leite, *A História da Companhia de Jesus no Brasil* (1938).

Born in Lisbon on 14 August 1629 to Emanuel Vilela Costa and Joana Gusmão, Alexandre Gusmão was baptized in the medieval Lisbon church of São Julião, an edifice that succumbed to the 1755 earthquake, was subsequently renovated during the Pombaline restoration, and currently belongs to the Bank of Portugal. Alexandre accompanied his father to Brazil in 1644. He enrolled in the Jesuit school in Rio de Janeiro, where he continued studies begun previously in Lisbon. Two years later, in 1646, having demonstrated his aptitude for a spiritual vocation, he entered the Jesuit Order. While in Rio, he followed the curriculum outlined in the *Ratio Studiorum*: humanities, grammar and rhetoric, and philosophy. By 1656, having transferred to the Jesuit school in Bahia, he took up moral and speculative theology, the crowning academic agenda of Jesuit pedagogy, reserved for candidates to the priesthood. He was ordained a priest on 2 December 1658, and thereafter taught in schools of the order both in Rio de Janeiro and in Bahia. His assiduous activities in the Jesuit system of education, both as professor and as administrator during the 1660s, helped him to focus his own pedagogical agenda, which began to emerge in his writings in the late 1670s (see note 7). He was twice provincial of his order in Brazil.

In March 1685, the order sent Gusmão to visit the villages of São Paulo and Santos. His mission was to mediate a dispute brewing between landowners and his fellow Jesuits regarding the indoctrination and social welfare of the

Fig. 2: Father Alexandre de Gusmão, S.J., pictured with the youth he loved and taught, from an engraving from Alfred Hamy's *Galerie illustrée de la Compagnie de Jésus* (Paris: Eget Forlag, 1893), now available digitally, thanks to the Raynor Memorial Library, Marquette University.

indigenous inhabitants. Twenty-four hours after its departure from Bahia, the Jesuit frigate carrying him was attacked by pirates. The boat's forty passengers were marooned on a deserted beach. Gusmão and associates saw the rescue of these cold and hungry passengers some six days later as miraculous. Gusmão believed that he had been saved for a purpose. His pirate ordeal seemed to harden our Jesuit's resolve to put into action his plans for the creation of a Jesuit boarding school, the generic first of its kind in Brazil. On 13 April 1687, ground was broken for the foundation of the Seminary of Belém da Cachoeira, which he would direct for several years as materials gatherer, contractor, architect, and, eventually, as its first rector.

By 1693, Gusmão, a man in his early sixties, had developed an extensive network among Brazilian society's elite and among his colleagues in the Jesuit educational initiative. When his friend and colleague Father Manuel Correia, then provincial for the entire Brazilian Jesuit community, died suddenly from yellow fever, Father Alexandre was his logical replacement. He held this office for another five years. Relieved of his duty as administrator of the Jesuit order in Brazil, he returned to his seminary in Belém da Cachoeira, where he was very much at home again as its rector, writing, teaching, ministering to his students, hearing confessions, and promoting the charitable Christian lifestyle so singularly championed in his allegory.

The Story of the Predestined Pilgrim:
An Allegory of the Ignatian *Spiritual Exercises*

Allegory is a literary creation wherein its author presents characters, places, and events, all interesting in their own right at a literal level, but which are susceptible to symbolic or figurative readings as well. Melville's *Moby-Dick*, for example, is the story of a whale hunt. But the vicissitudes of the narrative, its characters, the uniqueness of the white sperm whale, and the subtle ambiguities of Melville's own rich prose, have led readers and critics to call the work an allegorical examination of right and wrong, with the whale being seen variously as a symbol of evil, God, or, perhaps, an indifferent universe. Melville most probably meant his allegory to be an ambiguous one.

Permit a gross oversimplification of Dante's great work. The *Inferno* begins with a traveler lost in a dark woods. A dark woods, with its uncertain paths, crackling noises of branches dropping, and the wind moving through trees, is scary enough at the literal level. The reader is soon aware, however, that the dark woods is a metaphor for the unknown and the evil and sin that lurks therein. The more sure path that Dante's protagonist follows, on the heels of his faithful guide, Virgil, leads ever upward toward the light—yes, toward the light of day, but moreover, allegorically speaking, toward the light of moral and spiritual certitude and a reconnection with God. Dante chose Virgil to be his guide, perhaps, because he represents a transition from the classical Greco-Roman erudition of mythology to the birth and gospel of Christ, as anticipated in Virgil's fourth eclogue. Bunyan, who may not have known Dante's work directly, includes many characters and scenes reminiscent of the ascent through the inferno: the Slough of Despond, the Wicket Gate, Interpreter's House, Difficulty Hill, Palace Beautiful, Vanity Fair, the Giant Despair, Apollyon, and so on.

Now, on to Gusmão. On its surface, the colorful narrative of Predestined and his brother Reprobate is the story of two families moving from Egypt to their respective destinations. Predestined wends his way toward the New Jerusalem; Reprobate follows the primrose path to Hell, Babylon. The conflicts and seductions that ensue along the way, hyperbolized in the pages of Gusmão's prose, constitute a kind of morality play wherein readers are induced to identify with Predestined, hoping against hope, that they too might enjoy a sojourn to the hereafter similar to Predestined's, and, through that same reading, nourish an equally strong aversion to Reprobate's example. Gusmão's protagonists encounter a wide array of characters during their respective journeys: some beautiful, some grotesque, some honest, some conspiratorial. All are personifications of the virtues and vices, the good and evil that mortals encounter during their earthly sojourn. They flatter, cajole, entice, warn, threaten and instruct Predestined and Reprobate. Gusmão's expectation is that the more frequently, fully, and acutely his readers contemplate salvation and the paths that lead to it, the greater the probability that they will deal appropriately with the obstacles found in those paths.

But there is a more profound reading of the text. Gusmão's novel is an allegory of the *Spiritual Exercises*, authored and used by Ignatius Loyola in the 1520s, and circulated ceaselessly since: first in manuscript and finally, in 1548, in printed form. The Exercises were translated into English by Elder Mullan in 1914, and I refer to that edition, now available on the Internet.[17] Concomitant to the evolution of Loyola's thought and vision for a new and different religious order was the evolution of his Spiritual Exercises. They form a plan, usually constituting a four-week retreat, for a thorough self-examination in the form of prayers, contemplations, and meditations. An apprenticeship in the Spiritual Exercises, always mentored by a benevolent elder religious man—Dante's Virgil, Bunyan's Interpreter, Gusmão's Good Angel—was, and still is, integral to the process of becoming a Jesuit.

These Ignatian contemplations and meditations are to be, as one might expect, the vivid imagining of the horrors of Hell and of the delights of paradisiacal glory. For the duration of the retreat, these contemplations of good and evil occur in dramatic juxtaposition, providing a reciprocal enhancement of their respective matters—a *discordia concors*—to the contemplator. For example, in the first week of the Ignatian retreat, the neophyte undergoes a "particular and daily examen" during which he "asks grace to know" his "sins and cast them out." This is followed by a "general confession with communion." Thereupon follows a contemplation of his several sins, being the first four exercises. The fifth exercise, embraced as a pedagogical prod to permanently erase his sin, is a "Meditation on Hell." Ignatius Loyola was very specific about how this meditation was to be undertaken. After the Preparatory Prayer, there followed two preludes and five points. The first prelude invokes seeing "with the sight of the imagination the length, breadth and depth of Hell." The second prelude is a conscious exercise of empathy "for the interior sense of the pain which the damned suffer." The five points of contemplation involve each of the senses, respectively. The initiate is "to see with the sight of the imagination the great fires, and the souls, as in bodies of fire." This is followed by an imagined hearing "with the ears wailings, howling, cries, blasphemies against Christ our Lord and against all His Saints." The third imagination was "to smell with the smell smoke, sulphur, dregs and putrid things." The fourth, "to taste with the taste bitter things, like tears, sadness and

---

[17] See http://www.sacred-texts.com/chr/seil/seil15.htm.

Descendant in infernum viuentes Ne descendant morientes S. Bern.

Fig. 3: Perier's imagining of the "width and breadth of Hell."

the worm of conscience." Finally, the fifth, "to touch with the touch; that is to say, how the fires touch and burn the souls." The use of his imagination, then, for the Jesuit initiate, was a serious undertaking in which the novice mentally saw, heard, smelled, tasted, and touched Hell. I believe that Gusmão—a practitioner himself of the Spiritual Exercises for some sixty-five years, and convinced of their benefit—takes his readers, young and old, Jesuit or not, through all of these experiences as well. To aid the twenty-first century reader in the imagining of these imaginings, I offer the following plates as visual aids. They are taken from a work by Alexandre Perier, one of Gusmão's Jesuit contemporaries, who was not content with the ekphrasis of prose. Perier published his *Desengano dos Peccadores* in the same year as Gusmão's death.[18] The two Jesuits were colleagues, and

---

[18] *Desengano dos Peccadores Necessario a todo genero de Pessoas, Utilissimo aos Missionarios, e aos Pregadores desenganados, que sò desejaõ a salvaçaõ das Almas. Obra composta em discursos morais pelo padre Alexandre Perier da Companhia de Jesus, Missionario da Provincia do Brasil. Em Roma, MDCCXXIV. Na Officina de Antonio Rossis na via do Seminario Romano. Com Licença dos Superiores.* [The Enlightenment of Sinners, Necessary to all kinds of Persons, Most useful to Missionaries and to enlightened preachers, who desire only the salvation of souls. A work composed in moral discourses by Father Alexandre Perier of the Company of Jesus and missionary in the Province of Brazil. In Rome, 1724, at the

Fig. 4: Imagining the "interior pain of the damned."

TORMENTO DA VISTA

Fig. 5: The torment of seeing Hell.

Fig. 6: The torment of hearing Hell.

Fig. 7: The torment of smelling Hell.

Fig. 8: The torment of tasting Hell.

Fig. 9: The torment of feeling Hell.

both were interested in the graphic depiction of otherworldly scenes of Heaven and Hell.

To Gusmão's credit, interspersed with the verbal descriptions of the hell experienced by Reprobate in his allegory, the Portuguese Jesuit has provided us with some marvelous Ignatian *imaginings* of Heaven.

Gusmão's dramatic 1682 narrative, whose focus alternates between the fates of his two protagonists — now Predestined, now Reprobate — is a compelling allegory of Loyola's Spiritual Exercises, first introduced more than one hundred years earlier. Even the uninitiated reader perceives the allegorical importance of the tale of Predestined's vicissitudinous sojourn toward salvation in the New Jerusalem. But the reader familiar with the early evolution of the Jesuit order, I think, must read Gusmão's narrative as allegorical at two levels: 1) it is a broad stroke Christian allegory written for the benefit and instruction of all Roman Catholics, and 2) to the initiated Jesuit or student of the Jesuit order, it is an allegory of the Ignatian Spiritual Exercises, per se, and illustrates the formative moments of the novitiate, replete with graphic contemplations of good and evil, virtue and vice, heaven and hell undertaken by all novices during their probation.

Some Considerations about the Content of *Predestined*

The twenty-first century reader will consider Gusmão's use of Ethiopians to personify Sin, Wrong, and Evil as politically incorrect (I, 3). Of course Gusmão was using a personification that was popular throughout the Middle Ages, and whose vogue may also have been refreshed in Gusmão's mind by the abrupt expulsion of the Jesuit mission from Ethiopia in 1630, culminating a dialogue with the Portuguese that had endured for more than two hundred years. My translation is faithful to the original for those historico-cultural reasons.

In Part V, chapter XI, Predestined has progressed in spirituality to the point that Charity becomes his particular mentor. The Pilgrim pays a visit to her bower. Gusmão evokes the Song of Solomon in his text and has the Pilgrim drink from Charity's breast. The ecstatic rapture that ensues is a mystical union of Predestined and God. In other words, Gusmão's Pilgrim succeeds in experiencing during the course of his journey exactly what advocates of Ignatian spirituality hope to achieve through the Spiritual Exercises.

Many of the English treatises on Heaven are circumlocuitous exercises in hyperbole, grounding their text in a suggestion of what awaits man in Heaven, as Richard Sibbes does, making their declarations "by way of negation," rather

---

press of Antonio Rossis, on the street of the Roman Seminary. With the permission of Superiors.]

than by positive description.[19] That is, the reader is invited to contemplate the rather vague sublimity of Heaven by considering a city in which there is no misery, no vice, no sin, and so on. Gusmão, by virtue of his fictive approach, is not constrained by the threshold of the knowability of Heaven. Because he is writing a novel, albeit cinched tightly to the Bible and to patristic writers, he can take the Pilgrim—and thus the reader—down into a purgatorial bath, then out of Purgatory, and right through the gates of the New Jerusalem, past the angels, through the musical massage of celestial choirs, and eventually into the very arms of the Savior, with whom the Pilgrim personally converses. There follows a rivetingly intimate embrace, a personally guided tour of His library, and more.[20]

The Title

Gusmão's use of the word *predestined* in his title was not intended to be polemical, or to involve the reader in some new speculation about the nature of good, evil, and the foreknowledge of God. Nor should it invoke such speculation today. Gusmão underscores the importance of free agency throughout his allegory. My assumption is that he, like most Roman Catholics of today, accepted the concept of predestination as a mystery.[21] Something must also be said about the man to whom Gusmão dedicates his allegory: Saint Francis Xavier (1506–1552), known in his own day and reiterated by Gusmão as the Apostle of the Orient. One of the original seven founders of the Company of Jesus, Francis Xavier had endeared himself to the Portuguese. Portugal's King John III was thirty-seven years old when the Jesuit order received approval from the Vatican. The rapidly expanding maritime Portuguese empire (coastal colonies in Brazil, Africa, India, and Asia) saw the rise of contentions between local inhabitants and the imperialist interlopers. The king sent his emissary to Rome to request that Jesuit missionaries be sent to Portuguese territories abroad to convert souls to Christ and to serve

---

[19] See *A Glance of Heaven, or, A Pretious Taste of a Glorious Feast Wherein Thou Mayst Taste and See Those Things Which God Hath Prepared for Them that Love Him* (London: Printed by E. G. for John Rothwell, 1638).

[20] For critical treatment of Gusmão's novel, see Sarah Augusto, "Entre o céu e o abismo ou a *História do Predestinado Peregrino e seu irmão Precito*," *Máthesis* no. 16 (2007): 125–43; Mário Martins, "*História do Predestinado Peregrino e seu irmão Precito*," *Brotéria* no. 78 (1964): 697–708; Zulmira C. Santos, "Emblemática, memória e esquecimento: A geografia da salvação e da condenação nos caminhos do 'prodesse ac delectare': a *História do Predestinado Peregrino e seu Irmão Precito* (1682) de Alexandre de Gusmão SJ [1629–1724]," *A Companhia de Jesus na Península Ibérica nos secs. XVI e XVII—espiritualidade e cultura. Actas do Colóquio Internacional*, Porto: Instituto de Cultura Portuguesa da Faculdade de Letras, Universidade do Porto, vol. 2 (May 2004): 563–81.

[21] I am indebted to Nelson Minnich of the Catholic University of America, whose delightful conversation helped me revisit this truth and others.

as mediators in the problems that arose with local authorities. The first leader of that mission was the Spaniard Nicholas Bobadilla, who became seriously ill and could not serve. Ignatius persuaded Francis Xavier to take the mission. The Orient intrigued him, and thereon hangs a tale. Traveling usually in Portuguese ships, he preached in Goa and Calecut in India, and in many lands between India and Japan. He baptized an estimated thirty thousand souls. So Gusmão's thought as he wrote the title page to his allegory perhaps naturally turned to his great spiritual forebear, the Apostle of the Orient and first Jesuit missionary; for Alexandre Gusmão saw himself no less a missionary, through the publication of his allegory.

The Translation

From the perspective of textual criticism, Gusmão's three Portuguese editions present only minor problems. There are lexical and orthographic discrepancies, but they are not major. For my English translation, I have consulted all three editions. The 1815 Mexican edition appears to be the most correct in several passages, which leads me to conjecture whether Gusmão's original manuscript was recovered and used for that early nineteenth-century Spanish translation. I have sought to produce in my English translation a text that is dynamically equivalent to Gusmão's original Portuguese. Gusmão's style was called "classic" by a number of early critics, including Barbosa Machado. Because Gusmão was a master craftsman of his native Portuguese, the process of translating *Predestined* into English was a comfortable one.

During the seventeenth century in both Roman Catholic and Protestant countries of the Western world, writers, poets, and philosophers sought what today is called enlightenment. The more religiously inclined a writer was, the more focused his work might be on attaining some degree of spiritual enlightenment. The OED notes that the use of the word *enlightenment* is rare before the nineteenth century.[22] In Portuguese the words *desengano* and *desilusão* both mean disillusionment, the salvific process into which mortals enter when their behavior begins to focus on shedding the illusions of the world. This is the sense of the word as it appears in writings on or about the Counter-Reformation (especially in the Mediterranean countries). By the eighteenth century, French philosophes

---

[22] See: *Enlightenment*: The action of bringing someone to a state of greater knowledge, understanding, or insight; the state of being enlightened in this way. Also: an instance of this. *rare* before 19th cent.

Also 1621 R. Aylett *Song of Songs* i. iv. iv. 83 The Word, without the Spirits *enlightenment*, Is as good Seede sowne on vntilled ground.

Also 1669 Le Blanc in C. H. Spurgeon *Treasury of David* (1874) IV. Ps. lxxxiv. 13 His lightnings, that is his divine *enlightenments*, are best seen. (my emphasis)

had co-opted the word *enlightenment,* imbuing it with their own agenda.[23] Interestingly, Bunyan uses neither the word *enlightment* nor *disillusionment,* preferring the more direct quest for salvation. The problem for me, then, was how to render the concept of disillusionment of the world as spiritual enlightenment. In order to maintain fidelity to the original text, I have usually chosen to use the words *disillusion* and *disillusionment* where these words occur in Portuguese, despite the fact that twenty-first century readers, upon reading these words, may intuit some negative sense in the context of those words, some sense of sadness or frustration. Occasionally, then, and especially where Gusmão examines the concept of disillusionment at some length, I have introduced the word *enlighten* or *enlightenment,* although neither has an etymological counterpart in the Portuguese text.

---

[23] See OED: Enlightenment: The action *or process of freeing human understanding from the accepted and customary beliefs sanctioned by traditional, esp. religious,* authority, *chiefly by rational and scientific inquiry into all aspects of human life,* which became a characteristic goal of philosophical writing in the late 17th and 18th centuries. Freq. in the Age of Enlightenment (my emphasis). Also see Sharon A. Stanley, *The French Enlightenment and the Emergence of Modern Cynicism* (New York: Cambridge University Press, 2012), particularly chapter 1, "Enlightenment as Disillusionment."

The Story of the Predestined Pilgrim and His Brother Reprobate

In which, through a mysterious parable, is told the felicitous success of the one saved and the unfortunate lot of the one condemned.

Predestined Pilgrim and His Brother Reprobate

PART I

PROEM

No matter how long we persevere in this life, we are but exiles or strangers. For absent from our patria, which is Heaven, either exiled from it for the sin of Adam or traveling toward it through the merits of Christ, we live in this vale of tears as sojourners and wayfarers. Saint Paul tells us expressly, "*Dum sumus in corpore, peregrinamur à Domino.*"[1] What is important is that we make the journey toward our fatherland, that we know the ways that lead thereto, and that we search out its entrance. The example of the following story or parable shall serve you as a guide.

---

[1] In English, "While we are at home in the body, we are absent from the Lord." Henceforth, translations from Latin will be included in the notes without comment. Many thanks to Prof. Roger Macfarlane of BYU's Humanities, Classics, and Comparative Literature department, who oversaw the English translations of the Latin quotations.

CHAPTER I

Of the patria, parents, and family of Predestined Pilgrim
and of his brother Reprobate.

In a city in Egypt called Gershon, which means exile, there lived two brothers, by nationality Hagarenes, which means wanderers. They were descendants of Hagar, who wandered for she, being first Abraham's slave, was later exiled, despised by her mistress Sarai. One of the brothers was called Predestined and the other Reprobate. Predestined was married to an honest and holy woman named Reason. Reprobate was married to a corrupt and wicked female named Self-Will. They both lived in such conformity with their spouses that Predestined varied not one iota from what Reason suggested, nor did Reprobate do anything other than what Self-Will told him to do.

Predestined and his wife Reason had two children; one was a lad named Good Desire, and the other was a daughter by the name of Upright Intention. Likewise, Reprobate and Self-Will had two children: a boy named Bad Desire and a daughter called Twisted Intention. Predestined loved Reprobate as a brother should, even though the latter murmured against him and not infrequently did persecute him. But with his sister-in-law he would have nothing to do, nor did he permit his children to communicate with her, for he knew how dangerous it was to raise children with access to Self-Will during their early years. Predestined's children were brought up well as children of Reason; but the children of Reprobate were the poorly indoctrinated children of Self-Will, and therefore they did not get along with one another, often falling into contention.

Predestined's wife, Reason, was singularly beautiful; all who saw her and knew her (except for the blind) became enthusiastically disposed toward her. She had only two rivals, Obstinacy and Passion, the daughters of Envy, who were blind and could not see her, and therefore did not love her. Reason's eyes saw with such perspicacity that no lynx could equal her, for what Reason does not grasp, no other vision can discover. She went about with her face uncovered, without the makeup to which others are accustomed, for Reason needs neither rouge nor adornment, nor must she be covered up with any veil. She had the noteworthy grace of being able to pacify contention; because that which Reason cannot settle, no other authority can bring to rest.

On the other hand, Reprobate's wife, Self-Will, was of the worst condition, completely a follower of her own appetite; if contradicted in anything, she became exasperated immediately. She was blind in both eyes, as are all Wills; because of this she tripped at every turn and often fell. Notwithstanding, she was passionately loved by Reprobate, who was sensitive to her slightest vexation, and from that sensitivity sprang his constant state of annoyance with all around him.

Predestined sent his two children to learn the liberal arts in the School of Truth; in like manner, Reprobate sent his children to learn the politics of the world in the School of Lies. Predestined's children improved themselves with the study of divine letters; Reprobate's children were led astray with the opinions of Atheist, and they grew from bad to worse.

~

CHAPTER II

How Predestined and Reprobate resolved to leave Egypt,
and of the preparation they undertook for their journey.

Resentful of their tribulations in Egypt and of the deceits practiced by its inhabitants, Predestined and Reprobate, like the Hagarenes or pilgrims that they were, decided to leave Egypt, which is the world, and with their families look for another city in which to make their abode. As they were consulting on this question with their spouses, without whose counsel they took no course of action, the children of both men returned from their respective schools, reciting the lessons they had learned that day. Predestined's children spoke of the excellence of the holy city of Jerusalem as described by the prophets and underscored what David said, "*Gloriosa dicta sunt de te, civitas Dei.*"[2] The children of Reprobate repeated the grandeurs of Babylon to which the scriptures allude and principally the words of Isaiah, "*Babylon, illa gloriosa.*"[3] As this reasoning was indicative of the intentions and desires of each, nothing more was needed for them to resolve to leave Egypt for Palestine: Predestined to make his journey toward Jerusalem, Reprobate toward Babylon.

They prepared for their journey the way pilgrims customarily do. Their garb was that of Baptismal Grace; over their shoulders they placed the vest cut from the skin of the Lamb of God, called Divine Protection; on their head they put a hat called Memory of Salvation; they held in their hands the pilgrim's staff called the Strength of God, cut from a tree that grows only in Paradise. They put on sandals: one was called Constancy, the other was Perseverance. Their knapsacks were filled with Good Purposes. From their belt hung gourds called Heart, filled with wine they call Spiritual Comfort. Into their pockets they stuck three coins with which to buy necessities: Work Well, Think Well, and Speak Well. Thus forearmed, our pilgrims bade farewell to Egypt and all its hopes, and left through a door that opens only for departure but not for reentrance, called Renunciation of Everything. For those who resolve to leave the world shall do so never to return to it again.

~

---

[2] "Glorious things are spoken of thee, O city of God."
[3] "Babylon, that glory of kingdoms."

CHAPTER III

Of the first journey undertaken by Predestined and Reprobate.

Predestined and Reprobate left Egypt traveling along a common road called Life, one full of a thousand precipices that led to a thicket of trees through which they made their tiresome way. The thicket was called Entanglements of Life. Although to Reprobate this journey seemed brief, Predestined found it quite prolonged.

This thicket of Life was not devoid of beasts: wolves, lions, and foxes, which are the passions of life, and, in one way or another, they detained the progress of the pilgrims, who were followed by these animals almost their entire way and could not free themselves from the beasts until the very end of their peregrination. From this thicket they emerged into a very somber valley called the Vale of Tears that is found along the Way of Life. Reprobate found it delightful: its trees were pleasant; its flowers were fragrant; its fountains were fresh. He would have been happy to remain there forever had his son, Bad Desire, not reminded him of the delights of Babylon, and had not Predestined's own example left him perplexed.

Living in that valley were different sorts of persons from every station, of all ages and conditions. Some were occupied in gathering flowers that bloomed; others took water from the streams; yet others hunted birds that flew about. Still others spent their time climbing the trees that grew there. In these occupations there was much dissent that led to disputes and contentions. Only a very few of them, whose garb suggested they were pilgrims, tearfully repeated the words of David: *"Hei, mihi, quia incolatus meus prolongatus est!"*[4]

Our astonished Pilgrims asked one of those who cried to explain the mystery of such diversity. This man answered, "Only we Pilgrims know where we are; we know that this life is an exile and that this world is a vale of tears. That is why we dress like pilgrims and lament like exiled persons. Those you see otherwise occupied are those who call this life their fatherland and know this world as a place of delights. Those busy collecting flowers are those who seek only pleasures and delights in this world. Those taking the water in their hands are they who try only to gather riches. Those who hunt birds are those who are occupied with only vain and useless thoughts. Those who climb trees are they who seek the dignity of high places. They are all deceived and are journeying straight toward Babylon, for the majority of them are Reprobates."

Fearful of some accident or of falling prey to one of the wild beasts that infest the most common routes, the travelers sought from one of those good pilgrims whom they had found crying in the Vale of Tears some guide or counsel to protect them on their way. The man they encountered gave them a very strong

---

[4] "Woe is me, for my exile has become prolonged!"

dog named Resistance and another one, fast of foot, named Flight, both born of a very wise hound named Counsel—for these were all that Pilgrims needed.

From this Vale of Tears, they ventured into another valley or field, which was actually not a different one but rather a continuation, called the Vale of Opportunity. Although at first sight it seemed delightful, it was a place of bad air and worse climate, and those who there dallied for very long did perish.

Predestined was enwrapped in the contemplation of how to make his way through that region (a problem to which Reprobate was oblivious) when he was approached by an Ethiopian, old but strong, named Sin, married to a malicious Ethiopian woman named Wrong. They were accompanied by a host of relatives whose naming would be endless if we tried to name them all. No sooner had the Ethiopians seen the pilgrims in their district than they engaged them and abused them pitilessly. The only solution was to call to view the dogs Flight and Resistance, governed by Counsel, and with that remedy the pilgrims escaped to a high mountain called Victory, far away from the Vale of Opportunity. For it is only by fleeing from opportunity and resisting sin that true victory is found.

$\backsim$

CHAPTER IV

Of what happened to Reprobate after he became separated from his brother Predestined.

Reprobate was just fine as long as he followed in the steps of his brother Predestined, but things changed when they became separated. It happened that they were confused about which route to take—whether through the valley or along the mountain ridge, because the path through the valley seemed as dangerous as the way through the mountain seemed difficult—when all of a sudden they found themselves in the presence of two young men of extraordinary gentility. One was pleasing to the eye; the other was not. They claimed to be great cosmographers of the roads to Babylon and Jerusalem; one was called Good Angel, and the other was Bad Angel. They greeted the pilgrims in a friendly manner and asked, "Men of good will, whither do you make your journey?" Predestined answered, "Jerusalem."

Reprobate said, "Babylon."

"You do well," both replied, "for this flowery road leads to Babylon, and by and by this mountain trail will take you to Jerusalem."

Then Good Angel set Predestined on his course to Jerusalem, and Bad Angel helped Reprobate on toward Babylon.

Here is where the two brothers parted, never again to see each other. Reprobate set off happily through the Valley of Opportunity with his depraved family. Not far along the way, he discovered a town which made him most content, for surely it was very near the gates of Babylon. It proved to be the infamous City of Beth-Aven, which means House of Vanity, for though at first it appeared to be sumptuous, it was empty within or full of bad neighbors.

An ancient and incestuous old man named Deceit governed the City of Beth-Aven. He was married to one of his sisters, an old and adulterous woman named Lie—both children of the Devil, who is the father of lies and fabricator of deceit. None of the buildings in the city had foundations; all the neighbors were merchants; their contracts were all usury and simony; the coinage was counterfeit; virtue was hypocrisy; friendship—if not simply for convenience—was perfidy. In sum, it was a city in which Deceit and Lie governed the House of Vanity.

Reprobate was well received in Beth-Aven because he found there many of his own name, Reprobate. Likewise his children found many of their namesakes, Bad Desire and Twisted Intention; almost all in the Palace of Deceit carried these names. They gave Reprobate lodging in a House of Vanity, for all dwellings in Beth-Aven had this name. They dressed him according to the style of the land and, although it stung him in his conscience to do so, Reprobate abandoned the honest and holy clothing in which he had been dressed when he left Egypt—including the under tunic they call Baptismal Grace. Nevertheless he soon adapted to the vain garments and customs of the land and became in almost no time as big-headed as everyone else. Let us leave him here in Beth-Aven, where his vain thoughts took him, and let us see the progress of Predestined, for it is his steps that we should follow.

$\backsim$

CHAPTER V

Of what happened to Predestined after he left his brother Reprobate.

Good Angel guided Predestined through the mountain which in our language leads Far from Opportunity; even though it appeared to be stony in places, the road was nevertheless a more sure road. He followed along the only trail there was, called *Via Domini*,[5] or *Via Pacis*,[6] with the warning that he should never go down to the Valley of Opportunity because of the great risk of falling into the hands of that miserable folk who had given him so many problems earlier on. So that Predestined would not stray from the trail, which was somber because of the thick trees they call Cares of Life, the Angel gave him a large candle, called Inspiration, lit by a light from Heaven. This candle is made from a very pure wax, derived from bees, called the Powers of Soul that comes from certain flowers called Divine Letters—flowers that were transferred from Paradise to the

---

[5] "Way of the Lord."
[6] "Way of Peace."

garden of the Catholic Church, thanks to the efforts of its own gardener, who is the Holy Ghost. With that clear light and so holy a guide, Predestined traveled the Way of Peace, and several days thence caught sight of the beautiful City of Bethlehem, among the principal cities of Judea certainly not the one of least note and one in which all our goodness was born. He grew so happy at this sight that he could not contain the joy within his breast and exulted in the following words: "God save you, Bethlehem, City of God, House of Bread, Luminous Orient where the Son was born, Homeland of God, City of David! More blessed are you because Jesus was born in you than because David was born there! Joyfully I come to you. Joyfully receive me within your walls, as you joyfully received the Savior."

Predestined would have said more, but the Angel warned him that on the Lord's path to not move forward is to move backward, and that it was enough that it was the first city he had entered on his way toward Jerusalem—for it had also been the first city in which Christ lived when he came from heaven to earth before entering Jerusalem.

Predestined finally entered, and he stayed for a time in Bethlehem, where two daughters were born to him: one, very sharp and wise, he called Curiosity; the other prudent and modest, to whom he gave the name Devotion. Curiosity took Predestined to see the different quarters of the city: the squares, the buildings, and the memorable things of Bethlehem. He saw the palaces of Boaz and the story of beautiful Ruth therein portrayed. He visited Rachel's tomb. He stepped into David's lake. He visited the Valley of Terebinth, where David had decapitated the giant Goliath. He saw the Well of Bethlehem, whose water David had desired and later offered to the Lord.

In like fashion, Devotion took Predestined to visit the holy places sanctified by Jesus in his early life. He saw the inns built for pilgrims by Saint Paula in the places where the Holy Virgin asked refuge in order to give birth to the King of Glory. He saw the monasteries that she founded and the place where she lived. He admired the sumptuous temple resting on one hundred and sixty columns that Saint Helen built around the gates of Bethlehem. He saw the place where Saint Jerome lived near the grotto of the Lord, and just as Devotion was leading Predestined into that holy place, the angel intervened saying, "To see so holy a place one should first see mystical Bethlehem, which represents the earth, for after the Savior was born there, Bethlehem became the City of Disillusionment, and without Disillusionment one cannot safely make one's way to Jerusalem." The angel gave to Predestined a horse swifter than the wind, called Thought, with a very practical guide by the name of Pious Consideration. On this steed he entered the City of Disillusionment, or mystical Bethlehem, governed by a noble lord of the same name, Disillusionment, married to an illustrious and saintly woman named Truth.

∽

CHAPTER VI

Of the Palace of Disillusionment and what happened there to Predestined.

It took no more than a moment for Predestined to find himself at the doors of the Palace of Disillusionment. Whereupon Consideration showed him the extraordinarily capacious main door they called Memory of Eternity, which consisted of two openings through which all persons passed. These openings were Eternal Glory and Eternal Punishment. Above the main door, written on bronze plates, were the words, "*O aeternitas!*"[7] He went immediately into an open courtyard, where he clearly saw the heavens and the earth; this place was called Knowledge of the Temporal and of Eternity, and all those who were there had permission to speak about Disillusionment.

In the four corners of this patio were four arches called the Novissimos of Man, in which there were four open doors. The first was named Memory of Death; the second, Memory of the Judgment; the third, Memory of Hell; and the fourth, Memory of Paradise. Over each one sat a trumpeter called the Voice of Heaven who continually repeated, "*Memorare novissima tua.*"[8] Although this voice was heard everywhere, it was only upon those who had entered the courtyard through the main gate that the horror of the Memory of Eternity seemed to register. Over each of these doorways there was engraved in golden letters the words of Saint Bernard: "*Quid horribilius morte? Quid terribilius judicio? Quid intolerabilius Gehenna? Quid jacundius Gloria?*"[9]

Another door or passageway called Transition served Disillusionment; it led immediately to a narrow room called the Hour of Death, where Truth and Disillusionment abide and can always be found. Because it is so narrow and dangerous, almost all who pass move on to Disillusionment. Here Predestined noticed a most unusual thing: most of those who came through the four doors mentioned above became joyful and carried the Passport of Disillusionment on to Jerusalem. Only those who entered through the door Transition, or through the Hour of Death, became sad as well as disillusioned. When Predestined saw this, he attempted to enter one of the four doors and came easily into the chamber of Disillusionment.

This was a very large and spacious room, but not very sumptuous, because in palaces, where Truth sometimes dwells, Disillusionment is often not present. This room had four inner chambers where Disillusionment lived, depending on the season of the year. The first was called Childhood, and in the spring Disillusionment lived there. The second chamber was the Age of Youth, where he abode

---

[7] "Oh, eternity!"
[8] "Remember your destiny."
[9] "What is more horrible than death? What more terrible than the judgment? What more intolerable than Hell? What more pleasing than Glory?"

all summer long. The third was the Age of Virility, where he lived in the fall. The fourth was Old Age, his winter house.

One could see, as in the first inner chamber, or Childhood, that many left disillusioned of the world, as happened during the three years that the Virgin Mary traveled to the temple, or when the young Baptist spent his time in the desert. From the second chamber, or Age of Youth, came many young men, enlightened all; some went to the Carthusian order, others joined the Company of Jesus or other different religious orders.[10] From the third chamber, or Age of Virility, some entered the state of marriage; others, disappointed with a first marriage, rejected a second one. Only from the fourth room, or Old Age, did he note that there emerged very few disillusioned souls, because those who do not become disillusioned with the world in one of the first three ages rarely encounter such disillusionment in the final period of their lives.

Finally Predestined was able to see the face of Disillusionment. He was in an honest garb, but at times his clothing changed, for sometimes he looked like a king, at other times like a monk. He seemed like a Proteus, appearing in different forms — now an ancient, now a young man — to show that in all guises, states, and ages, one can find Disillusionment. His eyes were always fixed upon his wife, Truth, and not for a moment did he leave her side. He had as his throne the globe, or sphere, of the world on two axes, or poles, called Life and Death, which began its movement on the pole of Life and ended on the pole of Death. Because in this globe other movements could be seen which altered its course, all finally came to rest on the pole of death. On this world globe were written two words: "Everything, Nothing", which phrase, although Predestined did not understand it, Disillusionment explained easily, saying, "The whole world is *nothing*; on the other hand, nothing is *everything* in the world."

∿

CHAPTER VII

How Predestined came to speak with Disillusionment and the words he heard him say.

Good Desire was pressing Predestined to speak with Disillusionment and tell him something of his sister Upright Intention. He soon spoke with a venerable and very efficacious old man who seemed to be the majordomo of the house. Forthwith he was given an audience with Disillusionment, who, after scrutinizing the pilgrim, his clothing, and his family, soon enough knew him to be Predestined. Returning

---

[10] See my introduction. Occasionally I have used the word *enlighten* or *enlightenment* where the word *desilusão* (disillusionment) appears in the original in order to convey a more modern sense of its context.

his thoughtful gaze upon Truth, who was standing there beside him, Disillusionment asked, "Is there still in the world anyone who truly seeks to become enlightened through disillusionment? God has his Predestineds everywhere."

Words cannot express what Disillusionment said to the pilgrims who had entered his presence! To those who had come in through the first door, Memory of Death, he drew his argument from those words of Saint Bernard, "*Quid horribilius morte?*" written above, and said, reasoning, "What thing is more horrible in this life than death? Horrible because it *must* come. Horrible because we do not know when that will be. Horrible because we do not know how it will come. But the time will come, Pilgrim, when you who now hear this—now live, eat, play, and enjoy yourself—shall be dead, ugly, horrendous, lying under a gravestone. What horror for us to be alive today and dead tomorrow! If from among all of you, oh Pilgrims, only one would have to die, that mere certainty would be enough to disillusion you. Well, is that not right? Is it not with that conviction that all of you shall come to your end? How then can you not become completely disillusioned?

"And if death is horrible because it must come, it is even more horrible because we do not know when it will come. And how do you know, Pilgrim, that this year will not hold the hour of your death? What do you know about whether you will die young or old, whether today or tomorrow? For though it is certain that you shall die, it is most uncertain *when* you shall die. Christ, infallible truth, is telling you that in the hour you least suspect it, in this hour shall fall the day of your death. And if it is today—as it is surely possible—what shall become of you?

"Death, however, is not so terrible just because we know it *shall* happen or because we don't know *when* it will happen, but rather because we don't know *how* it will happen. How do you know, Pilgrim, whether yours will be a natural death or whether it will be a violent one? Whether you will have time to think about it or whether it shall be instantaneous? Whether you shall die in the grace of God or whether you shall die a sinner? And if yours is a violent one, if it is instantaneous, or if you die a sinner, what shall become of you? Your remedy for this uncertainty is to become disillusioned in time."

To those who had entered through the second door, Memory of the Judgment, he again spoke the words of Saint Bernard that were found over the door, "*Quid terribilius judicio?*" And again he reasoned, "What thing can be more terrible than the terrific judgment and tribunal of God at which all of us must appear at the moment of our death? Terrible because the Judge himself is an offended God; terrible because the accusers are Demons and our own conscience; terrible because the examination of our works, thoughts, and actions shall be exact; terrible because nothing can excuse our load of sin, nor can the sentence be appealed; terrible because not only will our guilt be judged, but also our virtue; and, finally, terrible because our sentence shall be one of two: either eternal salvation or eternal condemnation."

To those who had entered through the third door, Memory of Hell, he alluded to Saint Bernard's words, *"Quid intolerabilius gehenna?"* He pondered, "What suffering is more intolerable than that of Hell? Intolerable, because it is a place of eternal flames; intolerable, because of the company of Demons and the condemned; because of the consummate dishonor of being a slave to the Devil; because of the eternal exile from your celestial fatherland, because of your exclusion from being with the greatest good, which is God. So tell me, Pilgrim, *'Quis poterit habitare de vobis cum igne devorante? Quis habitabit ex vobis cum ardoribus sempiternis?'*[11] No one. So why have you not shed your illusions? Do you or do you not believe that Hell awaits those who follow vanity? If you do not believe this, how can you call yourself Predestined? And if you *do* confess this, why do you not open your eyes?"

To those who with joyful countenance had come through the fourth door (or Memory of Paradise) Disillusionment said, *"Quid jucundius Gloria?"*[12] Pleasing, because it is a place of consummate joy where the soul, as Christ says, enters into the joy of the Lord; pleasing because of the company of the nine choirs of angels and the blessed ones of Heaven; pleasing, after all, because you are in the very sight of God, of which all blessing consists; because of the knowledge of the mysteries of God and the secrets of Divine Providence; because of the attributes and perfection of God, among which a soul is not only joyful, but surrounded by a sea of infinite joy. So tell me, oh Pilgrim, whether life has held any joy comparable to those joys of Paradise? Here, all joys are brief and false; only the delights of Glory are true and permanent."

CHAPTER VIII

Of Predestined's other experiences in the Palace of Disillusionment.

Thus spoke Disillusionment to all those who had come in through the four doors to kiss his hand. And to make sure that they left his presence truly bereft of their illusions, he did not dismiss them from his palace right away, but detained them for a space of time in his house so that they might slowly consider the arguments they had heard and contemplate the examples of those who, protagonists of those same arguments, had seen the light. Meanwhile, Notice took Predestined down a narrow corridor called Transition that led to a tightly narrow room called Brief Life, guarded by an old and dreadful-looking doorman named Fear of Death, by whose visage Predestined was notably perturbed.

---

[11] "What man in this life would dare live for a year in that voracious fire of Hell? Moreover, who would live in those eternal flames for a whole eternity?"

[12] "What can be more pleasing than the glory of Paradise?"

Here, in an unusual painting, Notice and Consideration showed the Pilgrim the realistic portrayal of a dying man who was experiencing the terrible anguish of death and was about to expire.

He was surrounded by numerous family members who, instead of providing him relief, seemed to increase his agitation. Besides family, other neighbors were present, ones who customarily accompany the moribund. Among them were Pains, Cares, and Anxieties; but the ones who bothered him the most were a neighbor called the Devil Tempter and others who might have been the latter's daughters or the daughters of the moribund himself, called Memory of the Past, Memory of the Present, and Memory of the Future. The first showed to the sick man his sins, his vices, his vanity, and what little penance had been done for past vanities; the second reminded him of his wife, his children, his wealth, and the life he was leaving; the third reminded him of the accounting of all this that he had to present to God and showed him the doors of Eternity through which he would have to pass.

Predestined considered how this was a true representation of what would come to pass for him and for all of Adam's children. The doorman touched his arm and pointed to the words that Disillusionment had written over the painting. They said:

> Make sure in life that you've begun
> —Take this to heart and do thy part—
> What in death you will be glad you've done.

Notice pointed out to Predestined other paintings in the room, all painted by Disillusionment for the pilgrims' benefit. He saw Saint Francis Borgia who—disillusioned with life upon the death of his Empress—renounced the Duchy of Gandia and the Marquisate of Lombay to become a Jesuit. He saw the Roman coal merchant count who, at the news of his father's death, renounced his earldom and became a coal dealer for Christ and, by doing so, a saint. He also looked upon the ancient philosophers who, to further their own disenchantment with the world, ate and drank from skulls of the dead and eventually placed their tombs in the thresholds of their doorways.

His disillusionment was further enhanced as he looked upon portraits of all those whose sudden and disastrous deaths had taken them from this life: the two Herods, Agrippa and the one from Ascalon, eaten by lice near Antioch; Julius Caesar, stabbed twenty-two times; the senator Fabius, who choked on a hair; Anacreon, who choked on a grape seed; and Drusus Pompeius, dead from a pear he swallowed. Homer died of sadness; Sophocles of happiness; Dionysius from good news; Cornelius from a base delight; Salvianus in the middle of a venereal act. There were innumerable deaths portrayed that would be endless to tell; over all of them were these words written by Disillusionment in his own hand:

Death just might come unto thee. . .
The same as it has come to me.

From this room called Brief Life, Notice took Predestined to another salon
which, though incomparably more narrow, was called Ample Account and was
reached through a hall called Narrow Way. Even more dreadful than the first
doorman was the keeper of this room, called Fear of Responsibility. They found
here a number of portraits that Disillusionment had faithfully copied as the old
accomplished artist that he was. The pilgrims were much moved by them. Near
the entrance was that painting by Michelangelo of the Final Judgment with the
startling signs announced by Christ and the prophets, to which Consideration
(who also knows how to paint) had added the souls of one Predestined and one
Reprobate, before the Supreme Justice, one with a sentence of salvation, the other
eternal condemnation. To strengthen the resolve of the pilgrims, Disillusionment had written:

A just judge and judgment book
Exact accounts and rig'rous look!

On the other side was copied the story of the terrible judgment that God gave
in this life to Bishop Udo, wherein he heard these words from Heaven, "*Cessa
de ludo, quia Lusisti satis Hudo.*"[13] He saw a portrait of the monk that Saint John
Climacus writes about: he was taken up to the judgment in an ecstasy and was
so impressed by what he saw that he was put into a cell where he stared at the
ground and there remained, silent, for twelve years. Disillusionment wrote under
this painting: *Quid erit in judicio?* Which is the same as saying:

If a dream has caused all this to be,
What will happen when I see?

Along the border of the room were seen realistic paintings of those who had put
this question to the test and had abandoned their illusions. There was King Bo-
goris, who had seen this vision of the judgment, renounced his gentile state, and
was baptized. Saint Dositheus had seen the same vision and renounced the world
to become a monk. The abbot Agathon on this account spent three days and
three nights, eyes fixed upon some far off point in wonderment, without a word.

From this room, Ample Account, Notice took Predestined to a third called
Long Punishment, down through an easy passageway. It was not unlike the passageway to Hell, so it was called Broadway. The terrible old doorman to this room
was called Terror of Punishment. Here Consideration showed to Predestined a
painting of the punishments of those condemned among the eternal flames of

---

[13] "Udo, cease from thy games/trickery, because you have played enough!"

Hell, where Disillusionment had written David's verse, "*Descendant in Infernum viventes*," which means:

> If first the painting you do see
> Away from danger you will flee.

They saw other examples painted on the walls of those who had considered Hell, changed their lives, and became disillusioned with the world. They saw Saint Catherine of Siena, Saint Christina, Santa Rosa, and many other saints, both men and women, who had considered infernal punishments, either because they envisioned them or because they contemplated them, and undertook incredible penitence and admirable mortifications. They beheld the servant of Theodoric, Bishop of Maastricht, who had passed on but had returned to life by some divine will and astonished those who saw the change in his life. He said, "If you had seen what I saw, you would do even greater things." They saw the monk mentioned by the Venerable Bede who, having seen the pains of Hell, renounced the world to become a monk. When people remarked at his bathing in tanks of snow and at other extraordinary rigors, he said, "*Frigiadora ego vidi; austeriora ego vidi.*"[14] In sum, there were innumerable cases portrayed of those who had considered the punishments of the condemned and truly shed their illusions. Wishing to influence these pilgrims in this same manner, Disillusionment added this ditty:

> One soul only dost thou have;
> A second soul, thou hast not;
> If now thy soul you choose to lose,
> Then what shall be thy future path?

Notice took Predestined from this sad salon to a much happier one called Glory because of its similarity to Heaven. To get there one went through a narrow passageway; the Narrow Way they call it. Its gatekeeper was a joyful virgin named Hope. Predestined felt his spirits rise, for he had become tired of the fears he had seen, and he found the good words of Hope as pleasant as the rare paintings therein. The centerpiece was a painting representing the glory of Heaven with such living and pleasant colors that for a moment he thought he might be with Paul in Paradise. On it the following words could be read:

> He who would to Glory go,
> As God has bid us all,
> Must now begin to show
> New life, and life anew.

---

[14] "I have seen colder things, I saw things more austere."

Again they looked at the examples of all those who contemplated such glory and had given up the world. There was Saint Alexis, who left his conjugal union on the very night of his marriage to become a poor pilgrim for the Kingdom of Heaven. There was Charles the Great, who renounced his empire to become a monk, as well as many other kings, princes, and lords who, for the love of glory, renounced their kingdoms and estates and joined religious orders. Among them shines the special example of Saint Mathildis, daughter of the king of Scotland, with her four brothers, of whom one renounced his dukedom to become a pilgrim. Another, who was a count, became a hermit. And another, the heir of them all, became a keeper of cattle.

$\sim$

CHAPTER IX

How Disillusionment showed Predestined the illusions of the world.

Disillusionment took Predestined up to a very high tower, called Superior Consideration, from which the whole world could be seen, and from which, they say, the wise Solomon could see the deceit and the vanity of all things in the world when he said, *"Vanitas vanitatum, & omnia vanitas."*[15] Predestined took out some spectacles that he had brought from Egypt, called carnal eyes, through which things are seen very much other than they are, similar to the ovate and angular spectacles from Italy, which make one object seem like one hundred and make an ant appear as large as a lion.

Predestined put them on and through them discovered the whole world in its beauty, richness, honor, delight, and great variety of things. He looked upon all the four corners of the earth and admired the richness of Asia, the precious metals of Africa, the opulence of Europe, and the grandeur of America. He considered the elements and venerated especially the humid element with the immensity of its ocean waves and the beautiful currents of its torrential rivers. In the terrestrial element, he enjoyed the freshness of its groves, the beauty of its flowers, the variety of its animals. In the air he loved the numerous kinds of birds, the secrets of the winds, the lightning, the meteors. And in fire he found beauty in the force of its activity, the admirable nature of its generation. In sum, he appreciated the concert and order with which they all composed the universe.

He descended to look more closely upon the riches, which seemed to him most estimable, given the high regard in which they are held by men. How great a thing must be money, which all men obey! Seeing the honors, dignities, and benefices, he was most impressed with the favors through which the lords were obeyed, reverenced, and served. He said to himself, "How great a thing it is to

---

[15] "Vanity of vanities; all is vanity."

rule!" When he saw the delights, the deliciousness, the gifts, he judged them all to be in conformity with the nature of man, and he asked, "If this were not so, what would man be?" He examined all other things that the world loves and esteems, like beauty, valor, health, fame, and nobility, and he was satisfied with what he saw. He said with wonder, "Blessed is he in this life who enjoys so many things!"

Predestined was already forgetting what he had seen and thought about in the four rooms of Disillusionment and the many examples he had been shown. The eyes of his heart were becoming focused on present things and began to grow fonder of the vain and illusory things of the world, when his wife, Reason, and his children, Good Desire and Upright Intention, cautioned him to follow the footsteps of Disillusionment, who was by her side and had these harsh words for him, "What are you doing, Pilgrim? Do you forget your name and your profession? Pilgrims who are predestined do not customarily look at worldly things with carnal eyes, but with eyes of spirit. Leave these glasses for the Reprobates—whom the world deceives—and their vanity, for they see only with carnal eyes. You who are Predestined take these other glasses, which they call Spiritual Glasses, and with them you shall see the things of the world as they are, and not as they appear." He put on the glasses, which were as clear as crystal, and was amazed to see how different objects appeared.

The first thing Predestined gazed upon was Heaven; he became absorbed with its beauty, with the immense capacity of its sphere, with the infinite number of its planets, the harmonious course of its movements, and the marvelous virtue of its influences. He said to himself in his heart, "If the starry heaven bears such external beauty, what could the interior of the empyrean heaven be like? If the stars and planets are so beautiful, what must angels be? And seraphim? If so much beauty can be found in Creation, how beautiful must the Creator be?"

Suddenly he looked upon the earth and exclaimed, "*Quam mihi sordet tellus, cum Caelum aspicio!*"[16] The four parts of earth seemed to him not more than four grains of sand, its whole grandeur but a spot, all its beauty ash, when compared to the beauty of any star. And since these spectacles were of such a crystalline nature, he was able to penetrate the most remote regions, far from the eyes of flesh. He saw the grandeur of the reason that God had created man, in order to see him and enjoy him eternally; he saw the natural and the supernatural means that God created to bring this to pass; he saw the importance and the risk of salvation, and just how precarious we are, as though hanging by a thread from divine Providence. He saw the horrendous maliciousness of a serious sin, as well as the greatness and excellence of divine grace and of the charity of God. He saw the vigilance with which the Devil seeks our perdition, and the carelessness of men in such a serious business as that of salvation. He considered the duration of

---

[16] "Oh, how ugly earth appears to me when I place my gaze upon Heaven!"

eternal things, the brevity of temporal things, and the anxiety with which men concentrate their attention on them, and the negligence with which they seek eternal ones. All these things he found worthy of note and to be slowly and carefully meditated upon.

As he was fixing his sight on this that we properly call the world, there loomed before him a large monster, or monstrous chimera, whose features indicated it was the same beast that Saint John saw in the Apocalypse, with seven heads and ten horns, the face of a lion, the feet of a bear, and the body of a leopard. Horrified, the pilgrim asked Disillusionment what beast this was, or what monstrous chimera. "This is the world," he answered, "which, seen with eyes of spirit as you now see it, is nothing more than a seven-headed beast or chimera, which has no being other than the one men pretend or fancy that it has. This monster is made of three animals: bear, leopard, and lion. For the bear is the symbol of lust; the leopard symbolizes greed; and the lion is the symbol of vanity. Likewise this world, as Saint John says, is made up of these same beasts: Concupiscence of the Flesh, Concupiscence of the Eyes, and Haughty Pride. The seven heads are the seven deadly sins, and the ten horns are the ten contraries to the commandments of God."

"And how is it," asked Predestined, "that before, the world seemed so pleasant to me, yet now such a horrendous monster?"

"That is because," returned Disillusionment, "before, you looked upon the world with eyes of flesh, and now you behold it with spiritual eyes."

And that was truly the case, for now wealth seemed to Predestined what in truth it is—thorns, excrement. Honors appeared as mummery, satire, and children's games; delights were brief, sweetness was bitter, beauty was deceptive, worth was worthless, nobility was vain, opinions were vanity—the whole world an illusion, all devilish traps.

Then he truly saw how the world and its glory is a comedic farce that evanesces, an entr'acte that ends with laughter, a shadow that disappears, a vapor that evaporates, a flower that withers, smoke that obscures the vision, a dream bereft of truth. Then he saw how the world, contrary to Christ, despises virtue and esteems only vice; how it flees from the Cross and loves only carnal delights; how it seeks only illusory riches and despises true and eternal wealth. He saw how the world justifies its lies, believes its illusions, vituperates virtue, and discredits truth. And finally he saw clearly just how false the world's expectations were, how deceitful its promises, how only that which is eternal is true, and how that which is temporal is illusion.

～

CHAPTER X

How Predestined went to see the rocky hillside in Bethlehem,
where Christ was born.

By now Predestined had spent many days in the Palace of Disillusionment and his wife Truth, who, as we have said, governed the most holy city of Bethlehem, which, after the Savior was born there, became the City of Disillusionment. The two daughters born to Predestined here, Curiosity and Devotion, wished mightily that their father would take them to visit the holy stable in the rocky hillside where Christ—the good of all of heaven and earth—had come to earth to heal us all, for this was the season of the year in which pilgrims usually visited Bethlehem. That is what he did on that horse called Thought, given him by Disillusionment, and in an instant he found himself at the gate of the holy stable.

He met his daughter Devotion and, as fate would have it, the time of their visit coincided with that of the holy Bethlehem shepherds who were looking for the Word, born in that same hour to a pure virgin. In the midst of that company, he dared to look upon and worship the beautiful infant whose being emitted such rays of light and divinity that the thoughts and hearts of those who looked upon Him were held in suspension.

Predestined could naught but marvel at such a sight in that place. His mind and heart were a confusion, and he knew not what to say for he was overcome as he considered the majesty of the infant, but then his thoughts ran to the vileness of that rocky hillside; he saw the heavenly angels who worshiped the child together with the baseness of the animals that accompanied the scene. He came to his senses and, following the example of the shepherds, dared exclaim in the following manner:

"Oh, golden child! Oh celestial infant! It is not just chance that has brought you to be born in the midst of so much lowness though you are the King of Glory and the Lord of Majesty. It must be for an example to me and for my own Disillusionment. I am a poor pilgrim who, for your mercy's sake, calls himself Predestined. Through the world's ambush and deceit, I go in search of true Disillusionment. Where better could I find it than here in your holy stable, with you in your holy manger? Lord, grant me the freedom from illusion that I seek in this place, even as I see you born here."

Consideration interrupted Predestined, "Think about it, oh Pilgrim, you who stand in this holy doorway—you shall see who Disillusionment is, everywhere spelled out. Look at this holy child. To what end, you say, was the Godchild born in so lowly a place, if not to condemn the grandeur of the world? To what end in such vileness, humility, and abandonment, if not to condemn the vanity, greed, and ambition of man? Is it not an intolerable deception to wish to be great on earth after God was born here so small? Isn't his being born a child the same as saying—just like children, who do not distinguish between gold and brass, or between the vile and the precious—that perhaps the world ought to re-consider the distinction it makes between the two metals?

"Now the poor swaddling clothes he is wrapped in, what do they tell us to do if not to condemn the pompous fashion of our dress? The straw in which he was lain, what does it invite us to do if not to accompany Isaiah's disillusionment that all is hollow and vain, as straw, and to consider that all earthly glory, like a flower in a field, is withered by the breeze? Does the humility of the stable and the simplicity of his bed not condemn the illusion of those who, for so brief a life, construct magnificent palaces, procure bedding of silk, and ivory cots? And finally doesn't everything you see in this holy manger shout out to the ears of our soul that everything the world seeks is an illusion?"

To further convince the pilgrim, she concluded with words from Saint Bernard: "Either the world is wrong or this child deceives himself; this child cannot deceive himself for he is the wisdom of God; therefore the world is wrong, and all its followers are wrong."

Predestined could not resist the logic, so evident, which informed the argument of the pious and devout Consideration. His breast could not contain his heart, nor could his heart bear the emotion he felt, and, with tears in his eyes, his words burst out, "Oh, Sovereign Master of our souls, beloved Jesus! Let not the world nor its glory deceive me, for what more do I have in heaven and what more do I want on earth than You as the object of all my desires? Banish from my heart all other love, all other hope. Let there be no place in my soul for the illusions of the world, its vanity! For I have seen You born in your manger."

Thus resolved and enlightened with the blessing of the Lord, Predestined went to kiss the hand of Disillusionment and received from him his passport, which he hid away in his breast or in his heart, together with a bag of coins for the trip, a memorial of the prudent urgings of his conscience, and left a happy man to continue his voyage.

~

CHAPTER XI

Words of wisdom that Disillusionment gave to Predestined.

Since this world is a farce or comedic representation, everything in it is an illusion; only through serving and loving God can one ascertain truth.

It is as impossible to serve both Christ and Vanity as it is to love both riches and God, for he who said, "Blessed are the poor," said also that it was difficult for a rich man to enter heaven.

It is impossible for the head of a body to travel one road while its members travel another. Christ, who is the head, began his career in Bethlehem, which is the House of Disillusionment; we who are the members of His body, how can we travel by way of Beth-Aven, which is the House of Vanity?

If the world is an ostentatious figure that passes, just as true a one is that of either king or lackey, and the world befools itself in trying to distinguish between the two.

The grandeur of the world is like a shadow: the higher it goes, the more it disappears. Its riches are gilded, but not gold; how then can they be true riches?

The more one has, the more one wants; that which cannot satisfy cannot be good. How great was the misery of Ahab who coveted Naboth's vineyard!

If you must lose one of two things, it is worth more to lose a little than to lose everything; a little is all the world gives, and everything consists in saving your soul. Therefore, it is more important to assure your salvation by leaving little than by acquiring much and risking your salvation.

It is a huge deception to abandon the certain in exchange for the doubtful; today is certain, there is some doubt about tomorrow; therefore it is deceptive to put off until doubtful tomorrow the question of salvation, which can be surely dealt with today.

If we must die only once and not twice, it is impossible that our one death be a practice for another death; it is important to assure one good, timely death, for as we negotiate the only one we have, there is no first one and no second one.

It is not possible to find sweetness in bitterness; he who loves delights deceives himself and does not consider repercussions; you may regret your whole life the delight you enjoyed for one hour, and you will find bitterness where you thought to find honey.

Our greatest carelessness is the exaggerated care we take of ourselves; our first concern is for the body when it ought to be for the soul; the more time we spend primping and preening our body, the less we spend in feeding and beautifying our soul; unjust is this division, which is not even an equal one.

The hour of death is no less an hour of illusion than of disillusion, for although, if considered closely, it enlightens some, when considered at a distance, it deceives all the rest.

What ambitious soul could there be, and so imprudent, who would trade the Kingdom of Israel for the poor vineyard of Naboth? This is what the ambitious and the greedy do: they give up the riches of the Kingdom of Heaven for the riches of the world.

It takes a great man to conquer the world, but an even greater one to despise the world; for the former can succeed through the virtue of others, but the latter must rely upon himself. The former overcomes hearts overcome, in turn, by ambition and covetousness; in the second instance, true Disillusionment is what triumphs.

$\sim$

Predestined Pilgrim and His Brother Reprobate

PART II

CHAPTER I

How Reprobate continued his journey toward Babylon.

For some days, Predestined's brother Reprobate had been living in the City of Beth-Aven, which, as we have said, is interpreted as House of Vanity. He had grown tired, however, of the bad behavior and deplorable customs of its dwellers, and—influenced principally by his two children, Bad Desire and Twisted Intention—he decided to leave Beth-Aven and continue his journey toward Babylon. In consultation with his wife, Self-Will, and the Governor of the city, Illusion, and, above all, in counsel with that aforementioned evil cosmographer, Angel of Satan, he kissed the hand of his lordship, was given back his passport to Babylon, and resolved to make his way through the lands of Ephraim, the land of Reprobates, as Saint Paul testifies, *"Ephraim non elegit."* [17]

He traveled in the company of his family with his passport in his breast pocket, near his heart, which said, *"Vanitatem sequor."* [18] Not far along the way he discovered the metropolis of Ephraim, which is Samaria, as the prophet Isaiah expressly states, *"Caput Ephraim Samaria,"* [19] a land full of idolaters and sinners, where no credence was given to the true God. He showed them the passport he carried in his breast and was admitted not only as a foreign guest, but as a returning citizen.

At this time Samaria was governed by a wicked old Samaritan called Vice, married to an evil woman named Profanity. With such governors, it was little surprise that all the citizens were vicious and profane. The government of the city was looked after by three bad rulers whom Saint John called Concupiscence of the Flesh, Concupiscence of the Eyes, and Haughty Pride. They governed everything, the aristocrats and the people; what is more, they governed many priests, prelates, and justices, and even the governors themselves did nothing of any moment without consulting these three bad rulers.

Now where did Reprobate take up residence? In a high quarter of the city called Pastime, where there were no occupations other than gambling, laughter, and entertainments. Since the language he had spoken in Beth-Aven was the same as that spoken in Samaria, within four days he was accepted and regarded as a Samaritan like the others.

In Samaria two children were born to Reprobate and Self-Will, similar in every way to the others: a boy called Disdain and a girl named Esteem. As they needed to be engaged in some pursuit, Disdain chose eternal things and Esteem chose temporal things. They were so good at their arts that Disdain disdained everything that was eternal; he despised anything that was mortification of the

---

[17] "Choose not the tribe of Ephraim."
[18] "I follow vanity."
[19] "The head of Ephraim is Samaria."

flesh, prayer, or piety. He therefore could not abide the good, the modest, or the devout, and he made his company with delinquents. In like manner, Esteem embraced all that was temporal: business, goods, scams. Only pious things did she not esteem. For that reason, she visited no one other than the nobility or the citizens, and she never took notice of religious orders or set foot in temples.

These children were so loved by Reprobate, who, for their sake, forgot his own life and all that he should have been mindful of, spending every day with them. This was Reprobate's life in Samaria, tempered by Illusion's counsel. Now let us see where Disillusionment's counsel took Predestined.

CHAPTER II

How Predestined continued his journey toward Jerusalem.

The time he spent in the holy City of Bethlehem proved to be a boon to Predestined, for he departed thence so disillusioned with the world that nothing repulsed him more than life's vanity. Nor did he love anything more than the durability of eternal things. One of the most impressive things that brought to him this clarity of spirit was what he had seen in the small and holy crèche in Bethlehem. This thought would not leave his heart and memory, "God child! God born in a manger! God had not arranged to be born to this earth with pomp and grandeur but, rather, with poverty and humility, a sign that all of life is vanity and that the only thing one must seek and love is what God sought and loved." Therefore, resolute Predestined, with the pleasing counsel of his wife Reason and his children Good Desire and Upright Intention, and moreover because of the opinion of that good cosmographer, Angel of God, determined to make his journey through Nazareth, for they had told him that the straight way to Jerusalem is by way of Nazareth; thus had Christ our master done, when from Bethlehem, where he was born, he moved to Nazareth, where he lived so many years. He was called a Nazarene.

At that time there governed in Nazareth a good lord, pious and devout, named Divine Adoration, married to an honest and holy woman named Religion; therefore, all the citizens of Nazareth were religious, and Nazareth was the symbol of religion.

The mayor of the city was a kindly old man named Serve God; a pious, devout, and prudent man to whom Predestined showed his passport which he had received from Disillusionment. It bore the following words: *"Non erubesco Evangelium."*[20] These are the words of Saint Paul that a Polish prince, the brother of the Beatific Stanislau, ordered written on his tombstone. It is the same thing

---

[20] "I am not ashamed of the gospel."

as saying: I am not ashamed to be a Christian; I am not afraid to work the exercise of piety, to humble myself in prayer, to say prayers, and to attend church. For without this passport, it is impossible to live in Nazareth—that is, to live a spiritual life, piously and religiously.

Having examined Disillusionment's passport, Serve God gave to Predestined a stamp by the hand of his son, Good Desire, which would allow him to be admitted as a citizen of Nazareth. On it were these words: *"Dominum Deum tuum adorabis, & illi soli servies."* [21] For without this stamp, it had been decreed by Divine Adoration and also by Religion that no one could be admitted into the city. The dwellers in Nazareth were all servants of God, and all had come with this desire to serve.

Finally, Predestined went into Nazareth, and, because he was a novice in the land, he counseled with good old Serve God about where he and his family might make their home. Two boroughs in the city were pointed out, one called the World, another called Cloister, and into one or the other of these two sections fit all the city. In either one, it was suggested, Predestined could live piously and religiously. Predestined marveled to hear it said that one could live a saintly, religious life in the World, for he had always heard that religious persons were only those who lived in Cloisters, and not *in* the World.

"Ah, how wrong you are, Pilgrim," said Serve God, "For it is frequently easier to find more religious persons in the World than in the Cloister. 'True religion,' says Saint James, 'is a life pure and holy lived in the world (*inmaculatum se custodire ab hoc saeculo*).' Pilgrim, did you not read what is written of the religious man, Cornelius? *Vir Religiosus*, and of other women: *Mulieres religiosas?* And this, why? . . . if not because of the holy, religious lives they lived in the World?"

"What shall I do to be like them?" asked Predestined.

"It will be necessary," answered Serve God, "to go and kiss the hands of Divine Adoration and Religion in their own palace, for there they will teach you what you must do to live piously and religiously."

～

CHAPTER III

How Predestined visited the governors of Nazareth in their palace and what happened there.

Predestined went and saw that over the door to the palace called Abnegation there was a coat of arms in the shape of an earthly sphere with the words of Saint Paul: *"Nolite conformari saeculo,"* by which emblem the pilgrim understood what one could learn in Nazareth. For as the wisdom of the world is contrary to God,

---

[21] "The Lord thy God shalt thou adore, and him only shalt thou serve."

one cannot make the wisdom of God conform to the wisdom of the World. As he entered, he saw three statues or images that appeared to be idols, but because they were on the ground and not on the altar, he did not look at them very closely.

He found himself in the presence of Adoration and Religion, who were in a room that was very decent, clean, and well appointed. It looked like a temple. Both of them were on a throne that looked like an altar; they were not sitting, but kneeling, as someone worshiping the true God with much veneration. Once Disillusionment's passport and the stamp of Serve God had been recognized, Predestined was asked what he desired in that place. "To serve and worship the true God," he answered, "living piously and religiously in a borough of that holy city they call World."

"First you must renounce and detest three Idols that the whole world worships; they are found just inside the Abnegation entrance gate. The first is called Worldly Respect, the second What Will They Say? and the third, Self Interest; for whosoever serves and worships these idols cannot serve God nor give Him the adoration He is due. These are like those of Israel who wished to serve Baal and Astaroth, as well as the true God of Elias." It was then that Predestined understood the mystery of the statues that he had seen at the entrance, and why they were face-down on the ground and not on the altar: so that those new arrivals in Nazareth would tread upon them with utter disregard. Thus the possibility that they might be worshiped by those who did not know them was diminished.

But Predestined, although he felt disillusioned with the world, could not fully detest all the Idols; for he could not overcome What Will They Say? and Worldly Respect. In order that he might be more fully persuaded, Religion showed him a chair in the style of a pulpit, where there was a very pure, holy, and sincere Virgin — ornate, but not too ornate and not with the affects of vanity; in her hand was a small, three-stranded whip on which were written the words of Saint Paul to Timothy: *Argue, obsecra, increpa;*[22] in her left hand she held a Bible and a cross with the words *In omni patientia, & doctrina.*[23] In her mouth she had a trumpet with Isaiah's words: *Quasi tuba exalta vocem tuam.*[24] Near this Virgin were two others, very attentive, modest, and still. Both of them had ears on their breast and not on their head, with the words of Christ from the gospel: *Aures Audiendi.*[25] Besides these two virgins, there were many others that appeared less holy and prudent than the former. Rather, they looked like the five foolish virgins in the gospel, and they all had ears not on their breast as did the other two, but on their hands, on their eyes, on their mouth, some on their ears, and others on their noses.

---

[22] "Reprove, entreat, rebuke."

[23] "In all, patience and doctrine."

[24] "Lift up thy voice like a trumpet."

[25] "He that hath ears to hear, let him hear."

This looked like a monstrous thing to Predestined, for he knew very well from Philosophy that powers of a given faculty were not able to work the operations of other faculties without losing their essential being. But Religion explained the whole mystery to him.

"That first Virgin," said Religion, "is the word of God; in the form you see it, she teaches how one ought to preach. The two beside her, called Intention and Attention—and that is why they have ears over their heart—they are the ears to hear with, spoken of by Christ in the gospel. The others with ears on the other senses are those who hear the Word of God, either without paying attention or with the intention of seeing the gestures, hearing the voice, or feeling the talent of the Preacher, as well as of smelling the flowers that he preaches. That is why they have ears on their hands, their eyes, their mouths, and their noses. Since they are not bearers of true intention and attention, they have no ears on their heart, which are the ears that should hear the word of God."

Predestined marveled when he heard that explanation, and he asked Religion, "Tell me, Virgin, why is it not like this wherever the Word of God is preached? For I have often heard this Virgin, Word of God, most ornately decorated with pretty flowers, followed by copious throngs, but without the mysteries that I see here."

Religion sighed heavily and said to Predestined, "Oh, how deceived you are, Pilgrim! For that which you describe is not the Word of God, but Human Rhetoric. Even though it is *like* the Word of God, it is not the same, but something very other, indeed. What is the reason, pray tell, that in other cities of the world people do not live piously and religiously as they do in Nazareth, if not for the fact that in them the Word of God is not preached? Do you know, Pilgrim, that the fields of Christ are more threatened by the birds of Heaven than by the foxes on the ground? I mean to say that more damage is caused to the spirits of the faithful by the flightiness of preachers than by malicious heretics. Because the maliciousness of heretics is known, like the maliciousness of a fox, but you do not always know when a preacher is *flying*, like you do not always know when a bird is."

Predestined appreciated the reasoning of Religion and made a note in his heart to always hear the Word of God with intention and attention, as is required, and his determination spurred him in such a way that he resolved not only to abjure the three idols that we saw earlier, but he dared ask Religion just how he could put into works the words he kept hearing preached as the Word of God. To this question, Religion answered in two words: *gather* and *keep*. They seemed an enigma to Predestined; he thought he understood that Religion meant for him to "gather the fruit from sermons," and to "keep them." However, that fine old chap, Serve God, told him that, no, Religion had meant something else—although his understanding was not a bad one. "Remember where you are—in Nazareth," he said. "And remember what Nazareth means . . . then you will know the secret."

"Nazareth," answered Predestined, "means 'flowery' or 'kept.'"

"And that is exactly what Religion meant by those two words; 'gather' the flowers of Nazareth and 'keep' them, for in this is your salvation."

"Can something good come out of Nazareth?" responded Predestined.

"Come, and you shall see," said Serve God, and he took Predestined by the hand and led him through the streets and plazas of Nazareth, and in every one they found a garden full of fine and beautiful flowers.

CHAPTER IV

How Predestined went to see the City of Nazareth and what happened there.

He departed, anxious to gather flowers and fill a basket that he was carrying called Heart, when he was met by two diligent and sharp-looking young women that appeared to be servants of some great lady. Known by the names of Diligence and Disposition, they informed Predestined that no one could gather flowers except with their blessing. This was on orders from three women who were the guardians, or the gardeners, of the flowers of Nazareth.

"What are their names and where do they live?" asked Predestined. "They are Reading, Prayer, and Meditation," his companions replied. "And, although they actually live over in the other section, called Cloister, they can usually be found here in the borough called World by those who know where to look."

"It is true," they added, "that the Lord of this garden himself often distributes these flowers to those he wishes, and usually to pleasant-looking persons like yourself, with good children like the ones you have, Good Desire and Upright Intention. However, flowers are usually not gathered here, but only on order of those three women, Reading, Prayer, and Meditation."

He left in the company of the two sisters, Diligence and Disposition, and first visited the house of Reading. They found her absorbed in a spiritual book, living in a splendid library full of sacred books, all devout and honest. Not one book of comedies or novels could be found there, for such books should not be found in the libraries of Nazareth; I mean to say in the hands of those living piously and religiously. In order that pilgrims who entered therein might know how to behave and read the books in that library, there was a sign on the wall with the words of Christ, "*Quomodo legis?*"[26] Do you read for profit, or as a pastime? If it is as a pastime, it is time lost; if for profit, great will be the spiritual lesson you shall take from it, for as Saint Augustine says, "Spiritual lessons teach us to put off the world and love celestial things."

---

[26] "Why do you read?"

So that Predestined would remember to profit from the sacred lesson, they gave him a pair of reading glasses that consisted of two lenses, Attention and Consideration, made from a particularly diaphanous crystal called Understanding, or Concept, because if you cannot understand what you read, nor consider or understand the lesson, how can you profit from it?

From this house of Reading, Predestined went to the house of Prayer and Meditation, since they lived together, for they were sisters who wore the same color. Today they can no longer remember their own names; Prayer calls Meditation, Prayer, and vice versa. It was not as easy for Predestined to enter the house of these two holy women as it was for him to enter the first one, for he had to endure rigors and ceremonies.

He went and knocked on their door with a knocker called God's Vocation; when a quiet old man named Silence came out, he silently followed him back into a cubicle called Seclusion where he was delivered to a garrulous old woman named Supplication, who gave to Predestined a rosary of fifteen mysteries, several Hours of Our Lady the Virgin, and other pious books of prayer with which he kept himself busy in that first room. They called this the first Prayer Room, or Vocal Prayer. In it there were three closets or nooks called Imploration, Praise to God, and Thanksgiving, which had been cared for by two prudent, devout, and expeditious servants named Attention and Pronunciation.

After spending several hours in this room, he went in the company of Silence to another chamber guarded by a doorman named Readiness, who presented him to a saintly, humble, and reverent woman named Presence of God, without whose blessing one cannot enter into the closet where Prayer lives. Predestined became a good friend of this saintly Virgin, and from her learned the reverence that one must have to be in God's presence. "Oh, Pilgrim," said Presence of God, "if you were blind and they told you that a king was present, would not your human faith be enough for you to be respectful before him, even though you could not see him? Of course it would. Then even though you cannot see God's presence with your eyes, is it not enough for Divine Faith—which teaches you—to suggest you be in His presence with utmost fear and respect?"

With this instruction he followed Presence of God to another large room lined with doors or niches and devoid of any person whatsoever. When he asked what the secret of this place was, he was told that it was called Composition of Place. The doors were called Prayerful Matters, and that is why it was unnecessary for anyone to be there, for whatever door he knocked on would open by itself and within he would find Prayerful Matters. Predestined tried this. Hardly had he knocked on a door when it opened. Inside was a painting of a scene from the life of the Lord. Readiness strongly suggested that Predestined take it with him in preparation for when he might find himself with Prayer.

Finally, with the help of Readiness and the blessing of Presence of God, he was able to speak with the mistress of the whole Palace, who was Prayer. She was a most beautiful Virgin and beloved of God. She was clothed in flames to suggest the fire of divine love. She had a crown of gold on her head and a scepter in her right hand to show that she governs and ordains all things through Prayer. She had two wings to fly through Heaven, all the way to the Empyreal Throne of God. They were called Pious Affect and Devout Affect, to signify the essence and definition of Mental Prayer, which is an elevation of our mind to God by devout and pious affect. Once she was seen with a shield and spear in her hand, to denote that Prayer is an effective weapon against the enemy and an effective shield in infernal battles. Another time she carried a basket on her arm and a scythe in her hand, like a harvester, to show that Prayer is what cleans off the thorns of vice from the soul and gathers the flowers of virtue. She had three virgins near her through whom she governed and accomplished what she wanted; their names were Memory, Intelligence, and Will, whom, if she found them negligent or distracted, she woke up with whips called Acts of Faith. When these were not enough, the Virgin, Presence of God herself, put them in order, and when all of that diligence proved insufficient, she used other, rougher whips called Acts of Humility and Resignation.

So this holy woman Prayer saw before her Presence of God, whom she loved dearly, and recognized the story of the life of Christ, which Predestined carried with him and had taken from the room Composition of Place. With eyes fixed upon the ground and his heart upon God, he delivered up the painting to the first Virgin, Memory. She studied it briefly and, in turn, gave it to the second Virgin, Intelligence, who looked at it, studied it, and considered it slowly and with much discourse. The third Virgin, Will, grew impatient to have it, and when Intelligence delivered it to her, she hugged it with hugs called Purposes, so tightly that it could never again be taken from her breast, or better said, from her heart.

CHAPTER V

How Predestined visited the flowers of Nazareth.

Predestined, instructed about the way flowers were gathered in Nazareth—by virtue and authority of the three women, Reading, Prayer, and Meditation—wished now to descend into the garden and gather what flowers he could into the basket of his heart. He began with the Rose of Charity, the Violet of Penitence, and the Lily of Chastity. One of these Virgins approached him, saying that these were not the flowers he had orders to pick, but rather they would pluck just some carnations called Good Purposes, and these would be enough for the time being. The other flowers, which are the other virtues, can only be picked by those who plant them. Predestined should consider going with God's blessing to the holy City of Bethel which, interpreted, is the House of God, governed by Charity, or Perfection, and there he would learn how to plant and pick these flowers, for in that venue was to be found their appropriateness. Predestined accepted that instruction and began to gather the Good Purposes carnations. Just when his basket, or heart, seemed full, behold a stout young man suddenly entered the garden with his reading glasses on and, whip in hand, was chasing off some mischievous boys and girls who were trying to steal the flowers in the garden as though they were fruit, and they had actually come to focus upon the very flowers that Predestined had gathered into his basket. To Predestined's query about that mystery, the two sisters answered that the lad's name was Circumspection, and the glasses he wore were called Vigilance, his whips were Severity, the boys were Feelings, and the girls, Potential. If Circumspection did not look after them with Vigilance and Severity, particularly the more mischievous of the lot—Eyes, Ears, and Tongue—there would be no carnation left in his basket nor flower in the garden. Predestined wondered at such behavior and that such cautious tactics would be necessary just to pick a few carnations. Moreover, he marveled to learn that there were so many in Nazareth who for many years had been in communication with these two holy women, and still did not know how to pick even one flower. To this the two sisters answered that the cause of all that was because those persons had not entered the garden in their company, but rather in the company of two other similar sisters, Negligence and Sluggishness, daughters of Weakness and Bad Habit.

CHAPTER VI

How Predestined went to see another section of Nazareth called Cloister.

For days now Predestined had been living with his family in the borough called World. His daughter, Curiosity, begged him to take them to visit the other borough called Cloister, where many excellences were reported. He went with the blessing of Religion because without it no dweller in the World can enter there; the only one he took was Curiosity, leaving behind the rest of his family. Soon after entering, he breathed in the goodness of salutiferous air called Spiritual Relief or Heavenly Favors, and although sometimes stiff, pestiferous winds of temptation are found, they are fewer here than in the World, and they do not seem to wreak as much havoc in Cloister, for the inhabitants know how to guard against it with panes they put in their windows called Sense Guards, and others they put in their doors called Cloisteration. The fertile land is rich with flowers of virtue and fruits of good works, abundant with Waters of Grace and Celestial Bread with which all sustain themselves, because material bread is not much used nor are gourmet delicacies or fine foods indulged in, as is the custom in the World.

In terms of building material, the whole section is surrounded by three walls: the first one of stone, the second of silver, and the third of gold. The first they call the Wall; the second is called Keep the Commandments; and the third is Keep the Counsels. They hold these walls in such high esteem that the principal care of the government of this borough is to conserve and maintain them through the labor of its ministers and officials. That is why they normally seek out only the most diligent and resolute, for if this responsibility should be entrusted to some negligent person, what should become of the wall?

The door to the borough is called Resignation and consists of two openings: Resignation of Will and Resignation of Understanding. Over the threshold of the door on the outside is a globe of the world like a coat of arms or heraldic symbol, and on the inside one finds the same globe, but turned around to show that the Cloister is nothing other than the world inside out; the world right side out has to be outside the doors because if the World and its laws manage to get inside the Cloister, there would be no difference between the Cloister and the World.

The inhabitants of this borough are governed by one man or by those to whom his authority has been designated; all obey or respect him as if he were God, and without his permission they cannot visit other sections of the city, and even if it is granted, they cannot do so without the counsel of two very prudent women: Piety and Urbanity. All their clothing is the same, called a Habit; very decent, very poor and honest, and one can see in it all the vanity and scruples of their dress, for since their clothing is a hood of the original justice that Adam lost, and the Habit is a shroud in which the Nazarene was buried, it is great Nazarene vanity to celebrate the shroud, and to decorate it with a hood.

Wealth is held in common, and for a person to have something of his own is a sacrilege. Yet though they have nothing, they have all they need of the temporal, and thus free from the cares of temporal things, they can more easily work for eternal ones.

In their behavior they are much like angels, for the things they say, their conversations, are either godly or, in fact, with God; a mutual love, a fraternal charity, their names are those given them by either parents or brothers or sisters. Their time is spent reading and writing, pursuing virtue, or principally in prayer. Over the library is an emblem made of virtue and science with the words: "*Conjurant Amice*,"[27] but with this warning: virtue is on the right hand, science is on the left, to denote that in religion, virtue always comes first.

At their worship services they are very clean, and in this the inhabitants of the Cloister differ much from those in the World. In sum, they live in such harmony that many call this borough Cloister, House of God; others, Terrestrial Paradise.

If someone is not living like he should, they put him in a cell called Paternal Correction, where he is tied down with two strong cords called Fear and Love; the Love cord is soft, the Fear cord is more harsh. And if this does not change

---

[27] "Friendly Conspiration."

his behavior, they throw him out of the Cloister into the World through some miserable openings called Incorrigibles, much to everyone's sorrow and regretful augury, for he who cannot live in a borough of such good climate among such honorable inhabitants, how can he go live in the World where the air is not as salubrious, nor the inhabitants so saintly?

Predestined found himself uplifted by such religious and pious dwellers; he would have liked to stay there, but he knew that as a married man he could not be a Nazarene, so he departed for the World to be about his journey.

CHAPTER VII

How Predestined was instructed in matters of devotion and piety.

Predestined departed so edified by that company of dwellers in the Cloister that he proposed in his heart to imitate them as much as possible in the World. With that in mind, he returned to Divine Worship and Religion and asked them how he might live in the World with Piety and Devotion. Hardly had he crossed the Palace threshold when their Lordships asked him if he had just come from the house of those three women, Reading, Prayer, and Meditation, and whether he had been well instructed by them about the politics of Nazareth. For otherwise he could have no audience in the Palace. When he answered in the affirmative, he was received with notable warmth by Divine Worship and Religion, who gave him a stamp for the room monitor, a prudent, holy, and mature old gentleman named Counsel. He recognized the stamp as the same one found on the passport from Disillusionment, "*Non erubesco Evangelium*," that Predestined had brought from Bethlehem.

Counsel escorted the Pilgrim to two very saintly Virgins, who were governesses to all the novice pilgrims that came to Nazareth. Predestined was immensely gladdened to see two such excellent matrons because, although they were very old, they were a most lovely, beautiful, and pleasing presence.

Predestined asked them, "By your lives, oh holy Virgins, pray tell me your names and who you are."

"We," they answered, "are called Piety and Devotion, both sisters and beloved daughters of Divine Adoration and Religion."

"My purpose," said Devotion, "is to have a willing and ready desire for all that has to do with Service to God in his capacity as God."

"And I," added Piety, "for all that has to do with Service of God as Father or Creator."

"And what shall I do," said Predestined, "in order to live devoutly in your holy company?"

"The first thing you must do," they answered, "is to frequently visit the house of those three holy Virgins, Reading, Prayer, and Meditation. For even though we descend from Divine Adoration and Religion, who are our parents, our daily exercise and occupation is in the house of these three women, and it is to them, under God, that we owe all that we have and know."

Since in Nazareth everything was explained by flowers and by words, because interpretation flourishes, Piety and Devotion gave to Predestined a plant of such rare flowers and remarkable fruits that it looked more like an artificial bouquet than a natural plant. This plant was called Spiritual Life. Its root was called Grace; its stem, Fervor; its flowers, Desires; its leaves, Intentions. It was very much like that Tree of Life that God planted in the middle of Terrestrial Paradise; for even as that one brought life to the body, this one brought life to the spirit. And because Nazareth was, without doubt, the land where trees grew with written leaves, this plant had the following letters with the following insight: on the root was written *"Dei"* [of God]; on the stem was written *"Sanctus"* [Holy One]; on the leaves was written *"propter te"* [because of you]; on the flowers was written *"ex te"* [out from you]; on the fruit was written *"in te"* [into you]. This meant that this plant, or Spiritual Life, should be rooted in the Grace of God; its fruit, or works, should be those of charity; its flowers, or desires, should be born of God; its leaves, or intentions, should spring from the love of God; and all should proceed from the stem, or holy favor.

This tree had three branches, for spiritual life is also divided into three parts: the first branch is called Purgatory because it has the virtue of purging the soul of its vices; the second is Disillusionment because it has the power to invigorate the soul's proclivity toward the exercise of virtue; the third part is Unitive because it warms the heart and viscera in the love of God, the way any creature is accustomed to uniting with its Creator.

Predestined was most content with so beautiful and mysterious a tree, and begged the Holy Sisters to tell him what he should do with it, how he might profit from its fruit and flowers. They answered that for the present he should content himself with keeping it fresh and green—watering it often with a certain water from Nazareth which would be shown to him—until Spring, when it would blossom into flower and fruit. "And where shall I find this water?" asked Predestined. "Come, and you shall see," they said.

CHAPTER VIII

How Predestined went to visit the fountains of Nazareth.

Predestined went in the company of Piety and Devotion and entered a Paradise, or garden, they call Congregation of the Faithful, and once his Christian signs were recognized—a Cross on his forehead and Baptismal Character in his soul (for without them he could not have entered)—he was introduced to a beautiful Virgin, without spot or wrinkle, of Christ, Himself. She was the Spouse, who is the Catholic Church. She was dressed as a Pontiff: on her head was a tiara; in her right hand was a cross; in her left hand was a book with some keys; above the book was a chalice; above her head was a dove. The tiara signified Supreme Dignity; the cross meant faith; the book represented doctrine; the keys, power; the chalice, the sacrament of the altar that sustains her; the dove was the Holy Spirit that attends her.

Under her feet were many emperors, kings, princes of the land, and a host of military instruments and engines of war, which represent the triumphs of the Church and the exaltation of faith. Off to a side were certain impious men who appeared to be heretics and gentiles; the gentiles were outside the garden and the heretics were in it, but all were shooting their arrows toward the woman, with the intent of finishing her off and destroying her. From within the garden on the other side, however, were other pious men who, with writing quills, repelled the shots in such a way that she received not a wound nor felt a threat. These were the Catholic Doctors and Holy Church Fathers, who with their writings defend her.

With blessing received, Predestined declared his faith and went to see the springs and fountains in the garden and to obtain some of the water that Devotion and Piety had promised him, customarily used to irrigate that plant, Spiritual Life.

In the middle of the garden, there was a stone that looked like the one from which Moses had tapped water with his staff, but it was none other, as Saint Paul testifies, than that cornerstone, Jesus Christ, in which, among others, were seen four holes at the four corners of the stone, called Feet and Hands. On the right side there was a larger hole. From these five sprang so many other fountains that Isaiah called Fountains of the Lord, that even though men call this water from that stone, it is, in reality, the true blood of Jesus Christ.

The waters from these five fountains gathered at another stone with seven eyes, which, in my view, was the one seen by Zachariah, because out of those seven eyes came seven springs that they call the seven sacraments. Its water, that they call Sacramental Grace, derives from seven pipes feeding seven fountains, or royal fountains, that beautify and fertilize the whole garden in a remarkable way. The first fountain is called Baptism; the second, Confirmation; the third, Communion; the fourth, Penance; the fifth, Extreme Unction; the sixth, Order; the seventh, Matrimony.

The first fountain, called Baptism, through which one enters to obtain the others (for no one can drink of the other fountains without first drinking and washing in this one), emits a water so admirable in virtue that it can hardly be explained, because besides washing the soul clean of all spot, guilt, and punishment of sin—both original and present, it has the virtue, like an aquafortis, of etching the soul, impressing on it the sign or Baptismal Character, by which it can be known and counted among the number of Christians. Without this sign, one cannot enter Jerusalem; but with it, doors are opened for him so that if a pilgrim, during the whole time of his peregrination, kept the purity vouchsafed by this water, and did not dirty himself again with the mud of new guilt—on this merit alone, he would be received into Jerusalem. "Oh, blessed pilgrims who have found so marvelous a fountain!" Predestined now exclaimed. "And, oh, how many of my brothers are there in Egypt, how many friends and relatives make their way toward Babylon, having missed drinking from this fountain and having not bathed themselves in such healthy waters! How many in the thickets of Asia, Africa, and America, know not of this fountain and suffer thirst! How many, if they knew about it, like I do, would come, like I, to Nazareth to wash, to drink, and to be saved! And oh, ingrates, oh, foolish pilgrims, who, after being washed in this water, have chosen willfully to return to the dirt and mud of their guilt! Worthy are they of being counted among those who never drank from it, and, like barbarians, of being counted among the citizens of Babylon."

The second fountain, called Confirmation, emits a water that comforts the soul for its battles of faith, providing it with spiritual might against its enemies. It also endows another sign, or character, by which the soul is known as a soldier of Christ and confirmed in the register of its company. One cannot drink from this fountain without first washing in the fountain of Baptism. And if, by chance, after washing in the first, one again becomes besmirched, he must then first wash in the waters of the fourth fountain, Penance, in order to proceed worthily.

The third fountain by order—but first by dignity—is of such divine artifice that not even the tongue of an angel can truly describe it. The stone from which it is formed is the very Flesh and Body of the Savior, and its water is the very Blood that through five founts was spilled on the cross, though, of course, it does not appear to be, for it is always covered by curtains. These they call Species, or Accidents, but they are certainly more fully appreciated with Eyes of Faith. This fountain is called Eucharist, which means Good News, for in it is contained the fount of all Grace: Christ. When it represents the sanguine sacrifice of Christ, it is called Host; when it unites the faithful to Christ, as a member of the body to its head, it is called Communion; when it is the provision for the way toward Eternity, by containing in it the blood of Christ that opens to us the doors of eternal life, it is called Viaticum.

Besides the pipe of the Blood of Christ—which is the principal one, and gives virtue to all the rest—this fountain has two other water pipes. One of them is Sacramental Grace and the other is Grace of Sacrament. Water from the first has the virtue of beautifying the soul—of enriching it and of washing it many times over, although this is not its principal virtue. Water from the second pipe, or Grace of Sacrament, bears twelve virtues or marvelous effects, represented by those twelve fruits from the Tree of Life that Saint John saw in the Apocalypse.

The first virtue or effect of this water is that it, by grace, transforms those who drink it worthily into God; the second is to magnify the sanctifying grace; the third enlarges charity and with it other virtues; the fourth diminishes the fomites of sin; the fifth gives life, it restores spiritual strength and the delights thereof; the sixth gives strength to combat the enemy; the seventh lends virtue to travel toward eternal life; the eighth is doubly effective against sin—it gives grace to the inner person, and to the outer person it acts as a repellent to temptation by virtue of the blood of Christ it contains; the ninth pays for venial sins; the tenth redeems from inadvertent mortal sins; the eleventh pardons from the punishment of sin according to the disposition of the partaker; the twelfth compensates for fires of Purgatory when the sacrifice has been a satisfactory one.

Predestined was about to dive precipitously into the currents of those divine waters when he found himself momentarily detained by Piety and Devotion. They informed him that the waters of that fountain were of such rare virtue that for some they were remedy while for others they were poison; to some they brought life, to others death, according to the disposition of every man. Therefore, if the pilgrim wished to try the effects of its virtues, he ought first to speak with a certain experienced doctor called Examination of Conscience, for in this consultation he would soon discover the state and disposition of his conscience, in order to profit from those mysterious waters.

So that is what Predestined did. Examination studied his pulse carefully and found that he was lacking in disposition. He was given two prescriptions for this: one was called Immediate Preparation, the other Remote Preparation. Remote Preparation was this: after drinking from the fourth fountain, called Sacrament of Penance, he was to purify himself from two water jugs very similar to those of Cana of Galilee, with which the children of Israel purified themselves, both of which were filled with that same water from the fountain of Penance; they were called Contrition and Confession. The second prescription, or Immediate Preparation, was this: after having purified himself from the two jars of water from the fountain of Penance, he was to dress himself in the white clothing of grace and charity of God, which the Gospel calls Nuptial Clothing. This clothing would be ornately decorated to represent the exercise of all the virtues, and the more decorated this tunic was, the better would be this preparation.

The two sisters, Piety and Devotion, added a counsel to those two prescriptions, and it was that after Predestined had drunk, with both these preparations from the waters of that divine fountain, he should retire to a far off place and sleep for a space of time on what he has drunk, that is, he should spend time considering the mystery and Sacrament that he had received. They like to call this a postcommunion Retreat, for without this effort, the full virtue of this water is sometimes missed. For if one arises from having drunk it in and turns to the other business and cares of life, there is no time for virtue to communicate substance to the soul and complete the experience.

From this third fountain the two Holy Sisters took Predestined to the fifth one, called Extreme Unction. As he commented on what had happened in the fourth fountain of Penance, it being one of the most important, they told him that the fourth fountain sent its waters a great distance from there to the City of

Capernaum, which means Field of Penance, where Predestined could live if he wished and where he could drink deeply from its bitter currents. This fountain, Extreme Unction, was of oil and not of water, from which only those could drink who were sick and whose natural illness had brought them close to the hour of death, for only these does the oil help. Its principal virtue is to reinforce the soul in that last battle against the temptations of the Devil, and as this reinforcement comes by way of the grace it communicates, it also cleans the soul of sin as a consequence. Moreover, this oil has the virtue of bestowing bodily health on the sick person when such health might benefit the soul—but not in any other case. It also mitigates the activity of the fires of Purgatory, so many who passed on from this life without it were detained in those flames longer than they would have been had they drunk of this sacred fountain at the hour of their death.

He moved on to the sixth fountain called Order, which from seven spouts emits an oil that can be used only by those who are to be ministers of this great lady, the Catholic Church—three large spouts called Sacra and four called Lessers, so-called with respect to the other ones. The principal virtue of this oil is to impress upon the soul a certain character or sign in which is given the faculty of treating sacred things, and of constructing the springs and fountains of this garden, and, as superintendents, of distributing their waters among those who live in it. Since this power is so great, and this office of the greatest authority that there is in the garden, those who receive it must be men of science, virtue, and prudence, and all others must respect, obey, and esteem them.

From here Predestined went to the seventh fountain, the one they call Matrimony, whose waters have the virtue of causing greater grace to abound in them only who, washed in the fourth fountain of Penance, drank from the crystalline waters of the third fountain—or at least remained clean from the first fountain of Baptism that they had received. The water from this fountain also has the virtue of extinguishing the illicit fires of Concupiscence of the Flesh, conciliating and uniting the spirits of the spouses, making them be one in conjugal love and helping them live in a manner whereby they represent the Spiritual Matrimony of Christ and his Church.

So with these waters, or with the currents of these seven fountains, Predestined watered the plant called Spiritual Life that Devotion and Piety had given to him, seeking to keep it green until the time its flowers and fruit would come, as shall be seen.

CHAPTER IX

Of the rare examples of Piety and Devotion that Predestined saw
in Nazareth.

After spending time at the fountains and in tending to this tree, or Spiritual Life, Predestined went in the company of these two good sisters, Piety and Devotion, to the Palace of Divine Adoration and Religion, with the intention of seeking their blessing and continuing his journey to Jerusalem. Before doing so, however, Curiosity invited the Pilgrim to see some of the relics of the ancient Nazarenes: the ruins of their temples, the examples of their lives, that were the model for those who, in the law of Grace, later followed in their footsteps, living piously and religiously.

They saw the work of some ancient artist, a painting called the Old Law, wherein were represented those that as Nazarenes had consecrated themselves to the service and adoration of the true God, as Samson, Samuel, the Prophets, and children of the Prophets had done. Among these, Elias and Eliseus with all their school stood out like the sun and the moon among stars, and in their footsteps followed all those who instituted the monastic orders for adoration and divine service. In another, more modern painting called New Law, Jesus the Nazarene was foregrounded with his whole Apostolic College. In second place was the Baptist, with all his school on the shores of the Jordan or deserts of Nazareth. Discernable also were the Holy Fathers of the Egyptian and Theban Deserts who flourished at the time of Saint Mark, all of whom were very religious men and inhabitants of Nazareth.

But what most caught Predestined's eyes and heart was that beautiful, incarnate rose of Nazareth, or flower of the field—Jesus the Nazarene among those two virginal lilies, Mary and Joseph. Because there he saw how in that humble little house they had received this rose, made human flesh, how He had there hidden the fragrance of his example and the virtue of his power for thirty years, living in subjection to Joseph and his mother, Mary, in exercises of piety and devotion.

With such illustrious examples, Predestined became quite excited. He was already entertaining thoughts about living in Nazareth permanently, living like the others in holy exercises with Piety and Devotion. But Religion, who intuited his pious desires, called to mind, quoting Saint Bernard, that there was no exercise of Piety nor tears of Penance outside the House of Bethany, which is interpreted as the House of Obedience, and therefore that obedience was the best adoration one could give God, because it was even better than Sacrifice, as He himself told Saul through the Prophet Samuel.

Thus, thoroughly disillusioned and, at the same time, enlightened, he tried to make his way to Bethany, or House of Obedience, and, kissing the hands of their lordships, he bade farewell with their blessing. And so that he might not leave Nazareth, the land of flowers, without a flower, Religion gave to Predestined two carnations; to his wife Reason, two roses; to each of his children, a single flower. The carnations were called Fear and Love; the roses, Faith and Truth; and the single flower was an amaranthus called Constance. In similar fashion, Divine Adoration gave to Predestined a flower called Adoration, made up of three petals named Latria, Dulia, and Hyperdulia. To his wife and children, she gave each a lily called God Before. In the same fashion, Piety and Devotion, who had also been Predestined's teachers and instructors, filled his knapsack with interesting, pretty flowers, some still in the form of buds, called Good Purposes, and others already in bloom, called Works of a Good Christian. He was given many other similar flowers like Rosary, Devotional, Indulgence Medal, Reliquary, and Agnus Dei, because from all these things, like flowers from seeds, piety and devotion are born.

Counsel, who was the custodian of the Palace, also wished to be part of the send-off. He filled Predestined's hat and breast, that is, his memory and his heart, with beautiful, healthy daisies called Spiritual Dictates, that he soon shared with his family, keeping for himself those that were most pertinent, which, if memory serves, were like those in the following chapter.

CHAPTER X

Spiritual dictates that Counsel gave to Predestined
in the Palace of Religion.

There is nothing of greater worth in this life, nor of greater esteem, than being good. If that which is good is naturally desired, even more so must one desire to be good. This advantage conquers all others, for no other thing can be sought unless it is in the form of good.

Good is virtue, and no other thing is better. So why is it not loved; why is it despised? Miserable blindness esteems a man for being a good philosopher more than for being a good Christian!

One cannot esteem as good that which can make us bad; riches can make rich persons, but they cannot make good persons; honors may make us esteemed, but not virtuous. Only virtue can make us virtuous, and goodness make us good. Virtue never deceived anybody; goodness never brought ill to anyone.

He who is ashamed of doing good is ashamed of seeming Christian. The artist who is ashamed of his profession is either not a good artist or he despises the art he studied. As the polished article is the best evidence of a good professional, so are acts of piety the best argument for our faith.

Serving the king of the land is held to be a noble thing and is anxiously engaged in by his subjects; serving the king of heaven should be more so. In the palaces of kings, no office that touches the king is considered low, although out-side the palace it might be so; in the House of God, every action of Divine Ado-ration is a noble one and ought to be esteemed.

In all places virtue has profited those who possess it—profitable on earth, and profitable in heaven. Today Saint Louis is more esteemed as a saint than as a king; one more highly regards Saint Francis's knapsack than Caesar's purple. More glorious was Peter the fisherman than the emperor Nero, who persecuted him.

Often virtue is mistaken for vice by one who doesn't know. For this reason one must be discreet in one's counsels. Flee extremes; choose the middle road, and you will do well. Virtue is found in the middle road; vice at the extremes.

It is dishonest to rationalize living like a beast: a brutal life is one of vice; a rational life, one of virtue. For if reason always follows the dictate of reason, vice was always at cross purposes with reason. Only one thing has not the vice of beasts, and it is that a wild beast is domesticated with kindness, but vice with kindness becomes furious.

One thing is to live long; it is another thing to long endure. The virtuous person can endure little and live long; the vicious person can endure long but live little. A Christian's age should not be measured by how long he has lived, but by how much good he has done. One shall not count the moments of time, but the degrees of grace.

It is a foolish thing to esteem another's reputation more than one's own con-science. You are not holy because others say you are, but because you truly are. The virtue you have shall save you, and not the opinion others have of you. You are not good because others say you are, but because of what you are.

The making of good choices in a spiritual life comes from knowing how to love and comprehend; through these doors come into our soul all good and all evil. Knowing how to distinguish vice from virtue, the vile from the precious, that which is eternal from that which is temporal, and the creature from the Cre-ator, is where correctness lies, and therein the true love and estimation of things.

In any love there may be error, illusion, and happiness: in the love of tempo-ral things—error; in the love of men—illusion; in the love of God—happiness.

It is contradictory to love God and offend him, to offend him and love him too. The negligent Christian, yet still in the grace of God, loves God through his charity, and offends God because he is lukewarm; he is a chimera of contradic-tion that cannot endure long without losing what grace he has.

A Christian without Faith is blind; without Hope, a coward; without Char-ity, dead; without Works, a cripple; without Grace, a monster; without God, nothing. Faith is light; Hope is strength; Charity is life; Works are hands; Grace is beauty; and God is the whole being of our souls.

The Sacraments are a plank in a shipwreck: light in darkness; remedy to ill-ness; escape from danger; strength in the way to salvation; inspiration in depression; treasure in poverty; life in death; victory over temptation—yet all this is despised by those who despise partaking of them.

Those who despise them prefer to die than to partake of peace; they prefer illness to taking a remedy. The Sacraments are sound nutrition and remedy for the soul; it is desperation or at least delirium not to use them in necessity.

Remedies for the body are sometimes taken with difficulty, often with the spilling of blood and cauterization of the flesh. Nevertheless, anyone who loves his health is careful to take them, though it cost him pain and pocketbook; nor does he mind exchanging wealth for health. Why is it not the same with the health of the soul, when remedy is freely and effortlessly to be had in the Sacraments?

~

Predestined Pilgrim and His Brother Reprobate

PART III

CHAPTER I

What happened to Reprobate after he left Samaria.

Having forgotten about his salvation and the life of Pilgrim, who was pursuing his own course, Reprobate had lived in Samaria for many years, had adopted its customs, and was in every way a Samaritan. Yet, prompted by some inner voice, or, better said, constrained by his own depraved Self-Will, he decided to take up his journey again toward Babylon, without bidding farewell to Vice, the governor of the city. He had fathered two children here with his same wife, Self-Will: a boy named Willful and a girl named Freedom, by whose counsel traveling the Broad Way, called Freedom from Conscience, he decided to make his journey through the cursed mountains of Gelboe, which means puffed up, and by and by all the Reprobates descended into the lands of Ephraim, where they made their camp in the city of Bethoron, which, interpreted, is *Domus libertatis*, House of Liberty.[28] With such children and such counsel, where would Reprobate go if not to the House of Liberty, or Free Life?

At this time Bethoron was governed by a man of low quality, by the name of Appetite, married to a woman of the same blood named Fantasy. They were of so singular a mind that anything Fantasy suggested to Appetite, he put into motion. All the neighbors in Bethoron were named Willful, and it is unbelievable how misbehaved all were in the liberty with which they raised their children, all of whom took up the customs and behaviors of their parents. The judges and the courts did not use reason as their guide but, rather, Appetite, who governed all.

Reprobate presented his passport—which he had obtained from Vice, the governor of Samaria—to the mayor of the city, named I Want. It read: "*Sic volo, sic jubeo, sit pro ratione Voluntas,*" which in good romance means: "I do not govern myself by reason, rather by will." As soon as I Want recognized it, Reprobate was permitted without further ado to enter Bethoron, or House of Liberty, as another of its citizens.

It is not an easy thing to describe the celebration with which Reprobate was received, how much he was delighted by the land, or how intimate its governors, Appetite and Fantasy, became with him, nor how quickly he grew obedient to their laws. He changed his name— shedding Pilgrim—and was ever after known as Willful Reprobate.

From so much eating of common fruits, called Liberties, a leprous plague called Oversense, and in Latin, *Noli me tangere*, fell on the land. It worked its way so thoroughly into the people that they all became Oversensed. Of this malady

---

[28] In this context, "House of Liberty" implies House of Libertinism. Interestingly, the words *libertine* (*libertino*) and *libertinism* (*libertinagem*) would not find their way into Portuguese until the eighteenth century. Gusmão opted for *liberty*, as in "taking liberties," in the context of his Reprobate.

almost all the inhabitants of Bethoron died, since not even an old healer—the only one who knew its cure, Mortification of Will—was permitted to enter the city or dwell therein.

No place was more suitable to the marriage of the Reprobates than Bethoron, and here they had more children than they had in the previous two cities together. They had five sons: one named Willful; one Oversensitive; one was Thorny; one was Grumpy; one was Obstinate. They had, as well, five more daughters, very similar in characteristics to their brothers: one was Disobedience; another, Obstinacy; another, Impertinence; a fourth, Laziness; the last one, Relaxation, who was a spoiled, lazy, and distracted girl—one who deceived the young men and many an old man as well.

Thus, Reprobate lived in Bethoron with his family. His was a brutal life, just like the one that all his neighbors lived, letting themselves be ruled by Appetite and Fantasy, as though men were not reasonable creatures, as though they followed the doctrine of Atheus, or Epicurus, and were not Christian, as though they had no knowledge of the immortality of the Soul.

Word reached Predestined of how misguided his brother had become. They say that his eyes teared up and that he exclaimed, "Oh, Self-Will, thus you fly headlong! You bring us all evil; you bring us perdition. My brother Reprobate would not have become lost if he had not married you. How you have erred, oh, misguided brother, in following the impulses of Self-Will, and not the path of reason! Oh, children of Reprobate, how foolish is your behavior, and how cursed you shall be!"

∼

CHAPTER II

Of what happened to Predestined after he left Nazareth.

These were the steps trod by Reprobate; those of Predestined led elsewhere. He had fathered two more beautiful, pleasant children in Nazareth; a boy named Efficient Judgment, and a girl named Will Subjected. After counseling with them, he made his way along a royal road that David called *Via mandatorum*, the Way of the Commandments, which held no tripping stones nor any other risk, and would lead them straight to Bethany, which interpreted is City of Obedience, through which they told him he must travel and even live in if he wished to reach Jerusalem. For just as in Bethoron, or Free Life, Reprobate found his perdition, even so in Bethany, or in Obedience to Divine Precepts, is the salvation of Predestined to be found. Predestined entered the city and, moved by the entreaties of his two children, Curiosity and Devotion, mounted that horse we know called Thought, with Consideration for his guide, and visited the squares and places of interest in Bethany. He saw the Castle of Magdala, where those two saintly sisters Mary and Martha lived. He visited the Sepulcher of Lazarus. He worshiped at the Cenacle of the Lord, where He instituted the Altar Sacrament. Predestined walked through that room where the Lord had washed the feet of His Apostles and preached the Sermon of the Supper, and where the disciples of the Lord had received the Holy Ghost. He walked along the Jordan beaches where the Baptist had lived. He entered the house of Simon the Leper, where the Magdalene had poured her precious ointment on the head of Christ. Finally he explored the places that Christ our Lord had sanctified with his presence and enlightened with his doctrine.

During this time, as always, Bethany was governed by an illustrious gentleman from the royal household called Precept, married to a slave woman called Obedience: saintly was she, and loved by God. They were gladdened to see Predestined arrive in Bethany by way of the Commandments of God, and they requested an audience with him at the palace.

He arrived at the palace gates and saw over them in letters of gold the words of David: *"Beati immaculati in via, qui ambulant in lege Domini."*[29] Above the gates was a crier called Heaven's Warning who, with the voice of a trumpet, announced to all persons that traveled toward Bethoron with unchecked conscience, the words of Saint Augustine: *"Quo itis, homines, que itis? Peritis, & nescitis, non illac itur, qua pergitis, quo pervenire desiacratis, ad illud pervenire vultis, huc venite, hac ite."* This means: "Oh, miserable Reprobates, where does the impetus of your depraved will take you? That is not the way to Jerusalem, but to Babylon. If you wish to arrive at Jerusalem, you must enter here, for this is the only way."

Predestined made his way inside without difficulty and had hardly stepped through the doorway when he was greeted by a venerable lawyer, named Law, accompanied by the Chief of the Palace Guard and Magistrate of the whole district of Bethany. He asked to see Predestined's passport from Nazareth; without it he could not speak with their Lordships Precept and Obedience. From his breast he withdrew it, like another David; it read, *"Meditabar in mandatis tuis, quae dilexit:"* "Lord, I meditated upon your precepts, which I love."

CHAPTER III

Of what Predestined did with the governor of Bethany.

The palace and even the whole City of Bethany, or House of Obedience, were governed by two legitimate siblings named Observance and Observation. Observation was a mature old man who governed the rooms of Precept. Observance was a very capable woman who governed the rooms of Obedience, for if there is

---

[29] "Predestined are they who travel the way of the Commandments of God."

no Observation in one's leader and no Observance in one who obeys, then Bethany, or House of Obedience, cannot be governed.

Precept had on his head a crown called Prudence, and in his right hand a sword called Justice. In his left hand was a scepter called Power. On his eyes were glasses for close scrutiny as well as for seeing far away, called Vigilance. With them he was reading a book about Providence, and this book was resting on a stand called Rectitude. He had under his right foot an insolent young man named Carelessness, who was tied to a chain called Discipline; under his left foot he had a sly young woman called Dissimulation. She was restrained by another chain named Caution. Both of them were tied together by a chord of medium length named Behavior. Precept kept the careful eye of Vigilance on Behavior to make sure that it did not come untied or become frayed. For it was known that a girl named Relaxation (and it happened to be the daughter of Reprobate, born in Bethoron) was trying to gain entrance into the house of Precept and Obedience just to untie this knot or at least to stretch the chord to a length longer than necessary.

Predestined marveled to see Precept's tension and asked his lordship that same thing that another had asked Christ in the Gospel: *"Domine quid faciendo vitam aeternam possidebo?"*[30] His answer was the same as Christ's: *"Si vis ad vitam ingregi, serva mandata."*[31] Predestined answered that since he could crawl, he had been following this Way. He gave an order through his majordomo, Observation, that by way of Law, the Chief Palace Guard should instruct Predestined in the Way of the Commandments of God so that he would not trip or lose his way on it.

Law, however—and this bespeaks his wisdom and experience—thought that in order for Predestined to become knowledgeable about the Way of the Divine Commandments, it would be necessary for him to obtain a blessing from Obedience and live in her company for several days, listening to the healthy advice she customarily gives to those who truly seek the way to Jerusalem via the royal Way of the Commandments of God. For with lack of such experience or familiarity with the doctrine of true Obedience, many learned men instructed in Divine and Human Laws stumble and lose their way.

No sooner had Law said these words than—as it were, to underscore his logic—there was heard a great clamor of voices and the din of arms, as though from some great battle or contention. They ran to a window for a look and beheld two respectable old men fighting and stabbing at each other with swords drawn. The men were approaching Bethany and looked to be going toward the chamber of Obedience. One doesn't know if they were just clumsy or if it was their age, but what they were doing certainly did not mirror the rules of fencing.

---

[30] "Lord, what must I do to inherit eternal life?"

[31] "If you want to enter life, keep the Commandments."

Predestined was shocked and fearful of some ill fate; he asked Law, "Who are those old men, and how can they hope to be received in Bethany in the midst of such a quarrel?"

"Those old men," he answered, "are both sons of princes; one is Canon Law, and the other is Civil Law. They often quarrel, not because they are enemies, but because of the seeds of discord that idiots and enemies of peace like to sow among them. The sword of Canon Law is Censorship; the sword of Civil Law is Force, or Violence, by another name. Their awkwardness derives from either inexperience or from overzealous attacks. Their looking for a haven in Bethany means that until they can govern themselves by obedience to their superior, or by the rule and precept of their state—which is taught only in Bethany, House of Obedience; they will contend with each other, often kill each other, and be each other's undoing, in spite of their being illustrious old men and both worthy of veneration." And as further confirmation of the point he was making, Observation took Predestined up to a high tower in the Palace, called Providence, and showed him two roads—one going to Jerusalem, and the one that goes to Babylon—so that the Pilgrim could see for himself the pitfalls that await travelers not unlike himself, and might await him, too, should he not elect to stay in Bethany and live for a time in the House of Obedience.

He saw how many pilgrims traveled the road to Jerusalem, some with staffs, others without them; some with guides, some guideless. Most of those without guides or staffs tripped, stumbled, became lost, and wandered until they came upon the road to Babylon. Not one of them had stayed at the City of Bethany, but had skirted the city. Intrigued with their own adventure and not wishing to become needlessly detained in that city, they thought they would arrive the sooner in Jerusalem. These wrongheaded pilgrims showed that, guided by their own capriciousness and unwillingness to be subjected to the orders of Precept, they rely on their own strength and virtue and avoid the more sure hands of Obedience; these ramble off the road to salvation and are going directly to infernal Babylon.

But he saw how other pilgrims—those who took their guides and relied upon their staffs—were remarkably ahead of the rest, and how they rarely stumbled or lost their way, and how, if by chance they did, their guide put them back on the road, or their staffs saved them from a fall, or if they did fall, they were helped back up. Predestined noticed that these particular pilgrims had departed from Bethany for they wore the clothes used there. What this means is these pilgrims—those strengthened in the virtue of God and guided by the dictates of Obedience along the royal highway of Divine Commandments—are traveling safely toward the Blessedness of Glory, for as Saint Augustine says: "*Sola Obedientia palmam, sola Inobedientia invenit paenam.*"[32] When Predestined saw this, he tried to follow Law's counsel, and he went to kiss the hand of his Lordship,

---

[32] "An obedient man in truth speaketh of victories, because, when we humbly submit ourselves to the voice of another, we overcome ourselves in our heart" (Saint Gregory

Obedience, taking with him the two children that could be most useful to him. They were Efficient Judgment and Will Subjected.

～

CHAPTER IV

Of Predestined's audience with Obedience and what happened there.

Now Predestined found the apartments of Obedience, called Humble Heart (for that is the only place where Obedience lives), and entered, along with Efficient Judgment and Will Subjected, through the main doorway called Resignation, the only way in. There they found two small hatches, Humility and Gentleness, that were very easy to open. The whole house was guarded by that noble woman, whom we have met, called Observance.

Inside the apartment, or Humble Heart, stood Obedience, smiling and happy. Wings were on her shoulders and feet, like those of Mercury, and on her head a crown of flowers. Over her eyes was a veil. In her right hand was a sword of hardened steel; her left hand held a flexible staff. Whichever way she turned, there was a table before her eyes that held an open book; she was able to read better through the veil than without it. Under her feet a girl in very bad condition was trapped. Trapped behind her were two children, a boy and a girl who appeared to be siblings, held tight by a very strong silver chain. She had a dog in front of her and a hound in back of her; at her sides were two young dogs that she seemed to dote on.

Predestined marveled to see such a beautiful and venerable woman, one who was pleased with his children Efficient Judgment and Will Subjected. He said to her, "By your life, I pray thee, oh, holy virgin, that you tell me of your birth and who you are. And, pray tell, the secrets of so many adornments, for you look like one of Alciatus's emblems, or Pierio's hieroglyphs."

"That I shall gladly do," said Obedience, "since you are Predestined and desire to save yourself, and since your children, Efficient Judgment and Will Subjected, are so beloved by God and dear to me. You need to know, Pilgrim, that I had two births, both noble ones, of royal generation. The first one was natural: in this one I am the daughter of Holy Will and Rendered Understanding. The second is my mortal birth; by it, I am the daughter of Precept and Just Law. My condition is that of a Slave, for I was born to serve and to obey—not to be served, nor to command—and though I am a Lady and the Governess of Bethany, it is not by commanding, but rather by executing what Law demands and what Precept determines.

---

on Job, Aquinas Study Bible, https://sites.google.com/site/aquinasstudybible/home/job/ st-gregory-the-great-on-job).

"The decorations in which you see me adorned and armed are all attestations of perfect Obedience, with which I inform the pilgrims that come through Bethany on their way to Jerusalem so that they know how to recognize the road Commandments of God and how to get to it. Just from their names you will know their essence and properties, and therefore no explanation will be needed. First is the embroidered tunic in which I am dressed, called Simplicity. The veil at my eyes: Without Discourse. The Wings are Speed. The Sword in my right hand is Execution; the bendable Staff in my left hand, Docility; the Book from which I read is a compendium of all the laws, rules, decrees, constitutions, and customs of the Kingdoms, Magistrates, and Religions; the shelf on which it rests is Vigor; the miserable girl I have restrained underfoot is Repugnance to Precept; of the two chained youths, the boy is Self-Judgment and the girl is Self-Will; the chain is Subjection. The dog that goes before me is Care; the hound behind me is Happily; the two at my sides are Diligence and Perseverance. The crown of flowers on my head are the supernatural virtues that Pope Gregory speaks of—they bring to the soul true Obedience—and to show you that I am she, you see me thus, laughing and joyful."

So much wisdom amazed Predestined, and now he understood how true the statement was that said: He knows much who knows how to obey; now he knew how truly Saint Teresa had called Obedience a short cut to the celestial Jerusalem. And, above all, Predestined understood the vileness and miscreance of those who, for the world's recognition or for personal convenience, lose respect and courtesy for such a venerable Lady, and thereby dishonor and trample her progenitors Precept and Just Law and by extension the Law of God, whence all Law and Precept descends.

As though to confirm Predestined's thought—one knows not if by chance or if by some heavenly destiny—there was a great banging racket at the Palace gates. Observation moved to see what the matter was and saw, running pitifully toward her, an illustrious woman. As quickly as she was able, she found refuge in the house of Obedience, like someone fleeing from a wild beast, or like some wild beast itself fleeing from its hunter. She wore on her head a rich crown of gold and came in supporting herself on two walking sticks of lignum vitae. Pursuing her was an angry old woman who looked like a Harpy; she was being stoned by a passel of boys and girls. She was looking for safe haven in the house of some prince or powerful lord as a defense against such worthless ruffians, yet the old woman followed her right inside. She had been thrown out of her house that very moment by the very persons who should have defended her, so she had no alternative than to seek refuge in Bethany and find reinforcement in the House of Obedience. There, that Holy Lady defended her and freed her, because only she was able to.

Now a really flabbergasted Predestined asked Observance, "What woman is that? And who might those discourteous ruffians be?"

"That woman," Observance replied, "who flees persecution is Divine Law. The crown on her head is Dictate of Reason, which gives power to all laws. The staffs of lignum vitae on which she leans are Natural Law and International Law, on which the Law of God is grounded. That bad old woman following her is Law of the World, who has always fought with her; the young men and women who stone her are Human Respect and Reasons of State, because of whom disrespect is often paid to Law of God, which ought to be defended and supported by grandees and lords. But the exact opposite happens: as soon as they mingle with the Respects of the World, they lose respect for Law of God and begin to esteem Law of the World."

"Oh, how sure and true this doctrine is!" exclaimed Predestined. "How despised and trampled underfoot in the Courts and Palaces is the Law of God! How disrespected and trampled by these reasons! How often when Divine Respect meets Human Respect do we ignore the Divine so as not to miss the Human! How often for a tiny point of honor, for a chance glance from the king, for a friendly correspondence, for a dot of courtesy, for the nuance of aristocracy, do we tread heavily upon the divine law and diminish our respect for God! Oh, cursed reasons of state, how beyond reason you are! Oh, infamous Law of the World, how contrary you run to all the Laws of God! Oh, cursed human attentions, how worthy you are of being despised! Oh, perverse Law of the World, how many pilgrims have you turned away from the doors to Jerusalem? And for how many of them have you opened the doors of Babylon?"

∾

CHAPTER V

Of the rare examples of Obedience that Predestined saw in Bethany.

With what Predestined saw and heard in the apartments of Obedience, he was developing an affection in his heart for so holy and noble a woman. She encouraged this by showing him the rich paintings in which were preserved the memories of the most noteworthy men in Bethany, that is, those rare examples of Obedience contained in the holy histories.

First, on an ancient canvas they called the Old Testament, was a living depiction of Abraham sacrificing his son Isaac in order to obey God. There was also Captain Jephte sacrificing his daughter in observance of his promise to the Lord. Also there was King Moab with a sword over the throat of his firstborn son in view of the encampments of Israel for the welfare and salvation of its people.

On a newer canvas they call the New Testament were copied many of the natural examples of equal virtue or greater marvel. There was Maurus upon the surface of the water in the middle of the lake with no fear of drowning, saving Placidus by order of Saint Benedict. He saw the Abbott Mucius throwing his own son into the river in order to obey his prelate; the monk that Sulpicius refers to who threw himself into a fiery oven for obedience's sake, without any ill effects from the fire; the one who captured a lioness to bring to his superior; and other similar examples. In one section they saw Saint Bernard with Beatific Fr. Peter Caetanus, already deceased, who were ordered to cease working miracles, and they obeyed. In another section was that simple holy Abbess who commanded a certain obedience of already deceased sisters; they even arose from the grave in order to obey.

They were impressed by a holy virgin in the presence of two holy men, all persons of the cloth, who were energetically watering a dry stick as if it were some plant of great utility. The Pilgrim asked, "Who are those people?" "That holy virgin is the Beatific Livina Statense, who, for the space of seven years, had watered a dry stick on orders from her Abbess as a demonstration of her obedience; after seven years, it sprouted and grew into a beautiful tree. The two holy men were Abbott John and a monk, mentioned in Sulpicius, who had also watered—the first for a whole year and the second for three continuous years—on orders of their superiors."

The monk was there who had been writing and was called away on a matter of obedience and returned to find his writing completed in letters of gold. As was the one who was called away from a cask which he had left with the spigot open; upon his return, the spigot was still open, yet no liquid had been lost. The monk was there who had been conversing with Baby Jesus himself and had left to respond to the needs of his superior; upon his return he found the same Baby Jesus who said to him, "Because you left, I stayed; had you not left, I would have."

To further drive home the importance of obedience, they looked at some rare examples of Observance of Divine and Human Law that Obedience had copied by her own hand. They saw the seven holy Maccabeans who, before the example of Christ, preferred to suffer intolerable torments than to eat meats forbidden by the Law of God. Together with them was valiant old Eleazar put to torment for the same reason.

Then they saw a whole squadron of holy martyrs to whom tyrants offered honors, riches, and delights, if they would abandon the Law of Christ. They preferred to lose their lives by torture than abandon the Law they had embraced. They saw the examples of holy confessors and holy virgins, notably Saint Martin, now on a desert island, now throwing himself into the sea, now wandering the world, all in order to obey a precept; Saint Francisco on hot coals; Saint Benedict among the thorns; Saint Bernard in the snow; and the hermit Saint James on hot coals.

Finally, there was a painting that showed the three ages of the life of Christ: his infancy, his adulthood, his manhood. Over his infancy were the words: *"Exiit edictum a Caesare;"*[33] adulthood bore: *"erat subditus illis;"*[34] manhood had: *"usque ad mortem."*[35] Altogether this read: in birth, in life, in death, which meant at birth he had been born obedient to Caesar; in life he was obedient to Saint Joseph and his mother; in death he had died for obedience to his Father.

∼

CHAPTER VI

Of the preparation Predestined undertook for the Way of the Commandments.

Predestined was consumed with love for this holy woman, both for her beauty and for her holiness and rare life experiences, and for the stupendous miracles she had worked. Had he not encountered Obedience herself, he would have stayed in her company all the days of his life, for he had become persuaded that no life could be safer than that of Obedience. But because it was needful for him to move forward and continue to journey toward Jerusalem by order of Obedience herself, he went to kiss the hand of Precept and receive from him the orders that he should keep in the Way of the Commandments of God, whose route he needed to follow.

Precept consulted with Just Law, whose child he was and from whom he had learned all that he knew, and gave to Predestined the necessary orders that he should keep, closed and sealed with the seal of Fear and Love of God. He gave to the pilgrim a passport in which was written David's purpose: *"Meditabor in mandatis tuis, quae dilexi nimis."*[36]

Soon there happened a marvelous thing. Precept plucked his heart from his breast and, placing it on an anvil called Patience, he flattened it with two mallets called Tribulations, and when it was very wide and as thin as gold leaf, he wrote upon it the words of David: *"Viam mandatorum tuorum cucurri, cum dilatasti cor meam."*[37] The prudent governor wished to show the pilgrim that there would be no lack of work and tribulations in keeping the commandments, but that he ought not shrink, but rather enlarge the patience of his heart to go forward and keep them all.

Then he was asked to redo his clothing, his provisions, and his equipment in the following manner: On his pilgrim's staff, called Fortitude of God, he was to

---

[33] "There went out a decree from Caesar."

[34] "He was subject to them."

[35] "To the death."

[36] "I will meditate upon Thy commandments, which I have much loved."

[37] "Then, Lord, I have run the Way of thy Commandments when thou didst enlarge my heart."

affix an iron point called Insurance, meaning that only in the Fortitude of God was their [pilgrims'] Insurance, for he was not to confide in human strength or virtue. On his inner tunic, called Baptismal Grace, he was to sew a border called Final, understanding this to mean that by keeping the commandments he could be saved until the end of his first grace, and that by breaking them he would be lost. On his pilgrim's vest, called Divine Protection, he was to place another very fine border, called Protection of the Virgin.

On his hat, called Memory of Salvation, he tightly fastened a ribbon called Memory of Condemnation. Onto his sandals, called Constancy and Persever-ance, he was told to fasten other soles, called Caution and Vigilance, so that they would not be used up on his journey. The gourd he carried on his belt, full of Spiritual Comfort called Prayer, he had to top off with another similar liquor called Meditation. On the three coins in his pocket, called Work Well, Speak Well, and Think Well, he was asked to write three words: Holy, Sincere, and Cir-cumspect, meaning that to really keep the commandments well, his work must be holy, his thought sincere, and his speech circumspect. To the two dogs they had loaned him for the journey, called Flight and Resistance, was joined a third, very swift one named Soon—giving to understand that he should not spend much time in the arms of Opportunity and of Sin, but rather, as Soon as these were seen or felt he should Resist and take Flight.

∾

CHAPTER VII

*Of the journey that Predestined made along
the Way of the Commandments of God.*

Thus prepared for the road, the first thing our Pilgrim did before taking one step was take a drink of that wine, or Spiritual Comfort, called Prayer and Medita-tion, from his full gourd. But he had not taken four steps when he was rushed by three beasts or monsters commonly called World, Devil, and Flesh. In their sight he grew sore afraid, but by virtue of the comfort he had taken, he mustered the wherewithal to call forth his dogs—Soon, Flight, and Resistance—and was soon enough free from that first danger. A second drink brought him great cour-age for any further such encounters.

On his way he saw in the distance a famous Palace called Decalogue, built by the very hand of God. The entire structure was of marble, and it was divided into two halls. The first was called First Tablet and was governed by Love of God. The second, or Second Tablet, was governed by Love of Neighbor. Although the first was larger and the principal one, the second one was very much like the first, as Christ our Lord testified in the Gospel. In the first hall or tablet, governed by Love of God, lived three illustrious nobles: First, Second, and Third Com-

mandments, whose principal office is to honor God. In the second hall, governed
by Love of Neighbor, lived seven other Lords: Fourth, Fifth, Sixth, Seventh,
Eighth, Ninth, and Tenth Commandments, whose occupations are to seek in all
things ways to profit Neighbor. This is why they say these ten gentlemen are en-
cloistered in just two halls — Love of God and Love of Neighbor — because all
ten are found in these two rooms of the same Palace, that is, in the two tablets
of the same Decalogue.

Obedience had ordered Predestined not to pass this Palace without going in
and personally meeting these nobles. She certainly knew them, for they all held
her in such high esteem, and depended so much on her, that without Obedience,
they could neither live nor govern their own houses. So he entered by a narrow
gate called Obligation of Sin, guarded by a saintly virgin named Religion, who
watched over the three inner chambers of the first hall where the three nobles, or
first Commandments, lived.

Predestined entered the first room of the first hall and saw a venerable prince
of such majesty that he seemed more a god than a man, judging from the way all
revered and worshiped him. He was accompanied by three very beautiful virgins;
one was dressed in white cloth, another in green cloth, and another in fiery cloth,
and besides the insignias they wore to indicate their dignities, they each carried
whips in their hands and with them drove away a great number of wild beasts
that furiously were trying to enter the Palace to trample and terminate that great
prince. On the door was written by the finger of God: *"Diliges Dominum Deum
tuum."*[38]

Fearful again, our Pilgrim asked Religion the mystery of it all. She answered,
"That wise prince called Adoration of the True God and the three virgins, Faith,
Hope, and Charity — the principal virtues — fight and overcome the impetus of
these beasts, the most ferocious of which are Idolatry, Heresy, Witchcraft, and
Simony, which are the principal adversaries of this First Commandment."

"And what shall I do," asked Predestined, "to reverence, and serve such a
venerable prince?"

"The first thing you must do is drive away those beasts with those same
whips, or Acts of Faith, Hope, and Charity; next, you must try to do some kindness, offering him some of those flowers I gave you in Nazareth. First you should
offer him continually the two lilies, Fear and Love; then immediately the ama-
ryllis, Adoration, which as you saw has three petals called Latria, Dulia, and
Hyperdulia. The first signifies the adoration that one must have for God; in the
second is found the love one must have for saints and angels, friends of God;
and in the third is seen the regard which one must have for the Beatific Virgin
Mother of God, for that special holiness of hers which exceeds that of all the
saints and angels."

---

[38] "Thou shalt love the Lord thy God."

From this first room Predestined went on to the second, on whose door was written: "*Non assumes nomen Dei tui in vanum.*"[39] Inside lived the second prince, or second commandment, whose nickname was Name of God because His real name was ineffable and could not be pronounced. He was accompanied by two noble pages named Vow and Oath. Near them were three beautiful young women who appeared to be his daughters: Cause, Truth, and Justice — meaning that an oath, in order not to offend the Holy Name of God, must be just, necessary, and true. In like fashion, Vow had near him three other virgins who seemed closely related to him, without whom Vow could neither live nor exist. The first was Intention; the second, Possibility; the third, Liberty — meaning that for a vow to be good and valid, it had to be possible, deliberate, and of supernatural motivation.

At this door were also two horrendous monsters called Perjury and Sacrilege, who were trying mightily to force their entry and destroy Vow and Oath, the two pages of Holy Name of God. These monsters were, in turn, kept at bay by the Guardian of this first hall, Religion, or first Tablet of the Decalogue. She did this with two sharp arrows, Fear and Respect, for which those monsters nourished a healthy fear.

When Predestined expressed his desire to serve this prince as he had the first, Religion told him that the best service he could provide would be to guard the door so the monsters could not enter, that is, that he not offend the Holy Name of God by swearing falsely, nor commit a sacrilege by breaking a vow. From among the flowers of Nazareth, he should also offer this prince a rose called Reverence every time he heard that Holy Name pronounced. Moreover, should he wish to be a vassal of this prince without fear of disappointing him, he should become a close acquaintance of those three maids, Cause, Truth, and Justice, who were much loved by this lord, and without whom he could not serve the beloved page, Oath, but always a just, true, and necessary one.

Predestined went on to the third chamber, where there also lived a prince named Sabbath, and is now called the Day of the Lord — a happy prince, one that was particularly pleasant and peaceful; his nickname was Holy. He was in the company of three goodly maidens, Prayer, Devotion, and Piety, that find him especially holy. These virgins held bound in chains a number of persons whose desire was to profane him. To wit: chained by Prayer were some noisy young girls named Unworthy Works; Devotion held a mischievous lad named Arbitrary Outburst; and Piety held on to the most pernicious monster and greatest enemy of the prince, named Sin. The chain that held them captive was Keep. So some called this holy prince Keep the Day.

Moved by the example of these holy virgins, Predestined also desired to serve and honor this prince. Religion perceived his good desires and taught him

---

[39] "Thou shalt not take the name of the Lord thy God in vain."

that his best service would be to keep those girls, Unworthy Works, that rowdy boy Arbitrary Outburst, and especially that monster Sin, from ever entering the Palace. For on this Holy Day, or Day of the Lord, one ought to offer him flowers, collected in Nazareth, by the hand of those three holy maidens, who, for good reason, always accompany this prince. By the hand of Piety, flowers ought to be offered called Pious Works; by the hand of Prayer, others called Holy Prayers; by the hand of Devotion, a Book called Holy Sacrifice—and this Book, above all the flowers of Nazareth, is what most pleases this prince, particularly if it is offered through the good offices of Devotion.

These are the three chambers that Predestined visited in this first Palace hall, governed by Love of God, where by this metaphor he learned how to keep the first three Commandments of the First Tablet of the Decalogue, referring to the honor of God. Let us see how he visited the other seven rooms of the second hall, or Second Tablet, that refer to profiting his neighbor.

✑

CHAPTER VIII

How Predestined visited the second Palace hall and what happened there.

Predestined left the first hall, governed by Love of God and guarded by Religion, and entered the second hall, or second Tablet, governed by Love of Neighbor, which contained seven chambers where as many nobles, or Commandments, lived. Their entire purpose was to help neighbors in the same way as the first three sought honor for God.

As he entered the first room, he saw the words: *"Honora patrem tuum, & matrem tuam."*[40] Inside its door he saw a most delightful, courtly virgin named Piety arranged the way she is normally portrayed, with two children at her breast. She monitored the abode of Fourth Commandment, lord of this first room. When Predestined expressed a desire to see and serve this prince, Piety took him by the hand and showed him a shepherd, who, with his staff and crook, watched over his sheep.

Predestined was amazed that such a grand prince—lord of so noble a palace—would go and practice the office of a shepherd. He had always heard that those who dwelt in the house of this Fourth Commandment were the kings, emperors, governors, popes, judges, prelates, teachers, and lords, who, according to the doctrine of the theologians, were understood, by extension, to be the Father that in this connotation God commands us all to honor. However, so that all understand the obligations of the Fathers, which *they* are, and so that all understand the obligations of being sons and daughters, too, it is necessary for parents to *be*

---

[40] "Honor thy father and thy mother."

the Shepherd and for children to be the sheep. And in this manner they can live here and keep this Commandment to perfection.

"The Shepherd, Pilgrim, governs, sustains, and loves his sheep and watches over them," said Piety. "He corrects the error of their ways with his staff, and with his crook he defends them against the wolf. In the proper season, he shears their wool and when they need it, he cures their scabby mange. This is what a Father does who is a Shepherd: he governs, he sustains, he loves, he watches over, he corrects, and he defends his children; at the right time he clothes them properly, and when they are sick he nurses them, seeking like a Shepherd to keep his flock from going astray and helping them to find the straight way of the Law of God.

"In the same way, children defer to their parents; they should imitate the condition of sheep before their shepherd. The lamb is a most gentle animal and very obedient to the Shepherd. A lamb moves at the slightest touch of the Shepherd. It does not complain when it is shorn; nor does it squeal like the pig when its throat is cut. Thus should children behave their parents: obey their precepts, accept their punishments, and, like the lamb, neither raise their voice nor belittle the words of those to whom they owe obedience, love, respect—allowing themselves to be shorn and cut, that is, permitting their excesses to be shorn and their appetites to be trimmed. Like the lamb—with its wool, its milk, even its skin and flesh, which is all profitable to its Shepherd—so, too, shall the child succor his parents in the time of their necessities, not only with wool for their clothing, with skins for their shoes, with meat for them to eat, but even with the milk of their own child-rearing, when this is necessary."

Predestined followed on to the second room, where Fifth Commandment lived. The sign outside bore this precept of God: "*Non occides.*"[41] Inside, the governess was a very integral Matron named Justice, together with a prince in the form and clothing of a hunter. This did not surprise Predestined very much, for he knew that princes and lords were much given to the hunt. But he did not understand why the prince was dressed like a hunter. Justice told him, "In order to justly keep this precept, men must live together like a hunter lives with beasts.

"The hunter, Pilgrim, may not abuse or kill any animal outside his own district and preserve. And when he does kill one, it is not for hate nor for vengeance, but rather because he loves the animal that he kills, and this only after he studies the animal, aims well so as not to miss, and finally shoots. It is the same way in republics: only their lords have the authority of Justice to kill, and never for hate or vengeance, but only for love of public good, and only after the justice of that cause has been well examined.

"The animal followed by the hunter does not curse him, nor does it reproach the hunter. All it does is flee as best it can, escape his traps, and dodge his shots.

---

[41] "Thou shalt not kill."

Only when it has no other recourse does it turn and attack its pursuer, and then it tries to fight force with force. Thus we should not curse nor desire evil upon those who persecute us. The only thing we may do is flee their violence and avoid their traps. And when we have done all we can, then we may repel their force with force, letting our natural defense be a moderate one."

His lesson learned, Predestined moved to the third room, where Sixth Commandment lived. Over his door was the prohibition of the Lord: "*Non moechaberis.*"[42] A modest, honest virgin watched the door. She was dressed in clothing whiter than snow, which Predestined read as Chastity. Together with her was the lord of the house, in the custom and garb of a gardener, working tirelessly to clean and cultivate his garden.

Again Predestined marveled that such a noble prince would work in so humble and demanding a station. Chastity told him that these are the two principal things that must be done by those who wish to live worthily in this house with her: know how to humble yourself, and flee idleness through work. "Furthermore," she said, "No other activity can better serve this lord perfectly than to imitate the office and tasks of a gardener.

"The gardener, Pilgrim, digs and weeds his earth; then he fertilizes and waters the ground with what he draws from the well with the strength of his arm, when it does not fall from heaven. He puts a wall around his garden and defends it with his dog. That is what must be done to live here with me, that is, if you want to be chaste and keep this precept. You must mortify and clean the ground of your soul and heart of bad appetites and ruinous inclinations, fertilizing it or helping it with the understanding of your own weakness, planting in it the virtues necessary to do this. You must irrigate it with the water of penitence that you take from the earth of your flesh, by prodding it with the strength of mortification and above all with water from Heaven, which is the Grace of God, by the exercise of Prayer and the use of the Sacraments — not forgetting to surround yourself with a guard of caution, like the gardener, with a wall of circumspection. This you do so that those most dangerous and damaging beasts, Concupiscence and Opportunity, may not enter. Consider setting upon them the dogs you have with you: Soon, Flight, Resistance."

Inspired by those arguments, Predestined moved on to the next room, where they told him there lived the noble, selfless lord he wished to serve. He read over the main entrance these words of the Lord: "*Non furtum facies.*"[43] He found inside a prudent matron named Temperance, the mother of many, many holy virgins, and the legitimate sister of Justice, who often lives and abides in this room. Its lord was a merchant, and presently he was doing some bookkeeping, putting his accounts in order, discovering his debts so that he could repay them and not let Death catch him in his house with goods of others against the will of his Lord,

---

[42] "Thou shalt not commit adultery."
[43] "Thou shalt not steal."

for if that happened it would be stealing and not business. "And, Pilgrim, if you," said Temperance, "want to live with me in this house and serve this prince, you ought to do as you see and live like this businessman, with accounts current, weights and measures correct, doing everything you can to keep my sister Justice on your side—an accurate accountant whose office is to give to each his own."

From this room Predestined entered the fifth in order, where Eighth Commandment lived, in the uniform and office of a Public Notary. Over his door was this law of God: *"Non falsum testimonium dices."*[44] His doorkeeper was a very noble maiden of royal blood named Truth. When Predestined asked her why that prince was in such an office, being able—as princes usually are—to have their own secretary, Truth told him, "This must be the kind of person who lives in the House of Eighth Commandment.

"The Notary, Pilgrim," said Truth, "is obliged to take note of what he sees, and see well that which he takes note of—keeping secret that which he saw and took note of and telling no one save it be his Superior, and in the time allowed by Law. He takes an oath to speak the truth about what he sees and notices so that, under Law, it cannot ever be presumed that the Notary lies. For that reason everything to which he testifies before a judge is believed, even though outside the court his word might be doubted. And if you, Pilgrim, do likewise and conduct yourself like the Notary in what you see and notice about your neighbor, you will serve this prince well and surely keep this Commandment."

There were only two more rooms in the Palace of the Decalogue that Predestined had not seen. In them lived Ninth and Tenth Commandments. They were neighbors and brothers because they were sons of the same Will. Both were Fishermen: Ninth fished with a net; Tenth used a pole. These professions were well suited to their inclinations. Ninth Commandment's house was guarded by that virtuous virgin, Chastity, and Tenth's was kept by Justice—the same who watched over the houses of Sixth and Seventh. Ninth Commandment was throwing wide his nets, like the fisherman in the gospel who hauled in a large number of fish, keeping the good ones and tossing back the bad ones. "Pilgrim, that is what those must do who wish to live here," said Chastity. "The thoughts and desires you haul in with your net must be sorted: keep the good ones; throw out the bad ones. The fisherman cannot elect to bring in only keepers when he tosses his net. He cannot control whether poisonous ones are gathered in along with good ones; but it is in his hand to keep the poisonous ones along with the healthy ones or to recognize the poisonous fish and throw them back, like the fisherman in the gospel. You too, Pilgrim, may encounter bad and evil desires mixed among your good ones for salvation. But it is up to you to reject them when you see them, and not collect them for the vase of your heart. This behavior will allow you to live here, or to keep this Ninth Commandment."

---

[44] "Thou shalt not bear false witness."

Tenth Commandment was thinking like a pole fisherman about his line and hook, and he was very content with the little fish that God gave to him and which Fortune sent him to his hook. He did not covet what others caught, and he knew very well that their fish could not possibly end up on his hook. Nor did he even hope for the abundance of fish that high-seas fishermen brought home, nor for those that the net tossers collected, for he knew very well that pole fishermen do not catch so many fish, nor are their weak poles able to haul in great fish.

"That, Pilgrim, is how those who live here must live, or those who wish to keep this commandment. They must be content with what God gives them and with what their arm and their pole can catch, that is, with what their possessions and their station in life permit, without coveting or envying those of their neighbor's. Perhaps it will be better, Predestined, for you, who seek Salvation, to be a pole fisherman, than to venture forth on high seas."

CHAPTER IX

How Predestined visited the Palace of Human Law and what happened to him there.

When our Predestined Pilgrim had been instructed in the Way of the Commandments of God and appeared to have walked the Way sufficiently, he took his leave of the Palace. The first person he met was an old lawyer, schooled in both laws — respected by all Kingdoms and Nations under the sun. He was accompanied by a pageboy with a trumpet to his mouth. It was heard throughout the world when played. The old man was the Law of Nations, and the boy was Edict; the trumpet was Promulgation. It seemed to Predestined that the old man might be a very knowledgeable person from the way he was progressing on his journey. He asked the man if he might know if there was any other lord or lady along that road whom he might visit, for the way looked very long indeed. Law of Nations answered him, "Up ahead is the Palace of Human Law. There you will find all law, both human and divine."

Not far down the road, Predestined saw the gates of the Palace. Out to greet him came that Holy Virgin, Obedience, Governess of Bethany, in whose province and jurisdiction that enticing Palace was to be found. The pilgrim wondered how she could be here when she had her own house in Bethany, which is the House of Obedience.

The Holy Virgin said, "Obedience lives wherever Law lives." She said that its virtue was immense and that was why there were wings on its arms and feet, and why it dressed in veils.

Predestined was walking along with Obedience when suddenly he saw a man running, screaming, with whips in his hand, trying to rid himself of some boys and girls who, disquieted and seemingly against their will, went running out the door. Wide-eyed, Predestined asked Obedience what all that confusion was about in such a noble house.

The Virgin answered him, "The girls are Unscrupulous Opinions and False Interpretations; the boys are Customs or Abuses which bring a notable disquietude to the House of Human Law. That's why that young man, called Vigor, was chasing them out of the house with that whip, called True Sense, and the words you heard him shouting were his repetition of the text of Law: "*Ubi jus non distinguit, nec nos distinguere debemus.*"[45]

Upon entering into the sure company of Obedience, Predestined saw two august women standing, hands held, although one of them was, as it were, a step's height above the other one. One was dressed in green cloth, the other in red; both had crowns of gold on their heads and scepters in their hands. The one standing higher held in her other hand a three-edged sword, the other a three-bladed sword. Under the points of each sword there were two old women of dreadful countenance who looked like Medusa. Under their feet were two other beings who in their dress appeared to be female, but so disguised that only God could know their gender. Over the head of the woman on the higher step was a dove encircled with light that penetrated her breast, and on it were written the words "*a Deo.*"[46] From this brilliance, another ray derived that led to the breast of the other Virgin standing below on which were written the words "*ab homine.*"[47] Near both of these Princesses were a host of very ornately dressed young girls and also many prudent, honest young lads, all of whom seemed to be sons and daughters of those two Princesses.

All this would certainly have been an enigma or a puzzle to Predestined, had Obedience, so experienced in the House of Law, not explained the essence of this scene.

"The two Princesses you see standing," said Obedience, "are Ecclesiastical Law and Civil Law. They are standing because they are in force, holding hands because they help one another. Ecclesiastical Law is superior to Civil Law; that is why she stands higher. The crowns and scepters signify the power of both. The Ecclesiastical sword is Censorship; the three edges are Suspension, Excommunication, and Prohibition, with which the Law of the Church controls this old woman, Recalcitrance, you see under the point of the sword. The sword of the other woman is Fortitude; its blades are Punishment and Penance, with which the old woman beneath her, called Violence, is controlled. The two unknown women under their feet are Consciences to show that all of Human Law—both Ecclesiastical and Civil—can obligate our consciences under constraint of sin.

---

[45] "Where the law does not distinguish, we ought not to distinguish."
[46] "From God."
[47] "From man."

"The Dove and the ray of light that pierces their breasts is the Holy Ghost and Light of Heaven whereby the Legislator is governed. The young men and women you see are sons and daughters of both Laws. The children of Ecclesiastical Law are Decretal Epistles; the children of Civil Law are Digests. Anything that offends or bothers them, offends and bothers their mothers; therefore they are avenged."

Predestined stood dumbfounded at what he saw and heard and was clearly desirous of living in that house without offending anyone.

"What should I do to serve and please that Prince," he asked Obedience, "so as not to offend such beautiful and comely children?"

Obedience answered him with these brief words, "Pilgrim, you be sure to have me always in your company, for I am the one who governs and guards all Human Law. You may also take my two servants, Simplicity and Sincerity, for your constant companions while you are here, and you will do well. Now, because of the uncertainties of life, they may not always be with you; take this promissory note from my hand, to be opened when necessary, and let it be a reminder of dictates that on occasion will serve you well."

∽

CHAPTER X

Some dictates of Obedience and Observance.

The Kingdom of Heaven: some seize it, others steal it, some inherit it, others take it freely. Martyrs seize it, Confessors steal it, the rich buy it, the poor inherit it, and innocent children take it freely. But in the end, only the obedient in all those groups enter therein, for it is through obedience that all are assured.

There are two royal ways to Heaven: one is bloody; one is milky. By the Milky Way go the obedient; down the other road go all the rest.

They say that it is a more sure thing to take counsel than to give it. It is better to obey than to command. The way of those who command is full of danger and, in Holy Scripture, full of threats; but the way of the obedient holds neither danger nor threat.

Only the obedient can make virtue from vice, worth from guilt, prudence from audacity, valor from temerity—fulfilling with mere obedience that which some Superior may command with malicious or fearful intention.

The blinder the obedient, the closer he fits the precept; for if a lesser has no eyes with which to obey, then the Superior must needs be an Argos in order to command.

The more obscure the sight of the obedient, the closer he will hit the mark, for he is seeing with the eyes of God, which cannot err; for, measuring his step according to the Superior who stands in place of God, he does not what his own judgment tells him, but what God, through his Superior, commands him to do.

A blind man does not lead another blind man lest they both run the risk of falling in a ditch. But Will, which is blind, cannot be guided, without risk of falling, other than by another blind man—perfect obedience.

Make and undo all the kingdoms of the world, like the servants of Achab; run and encircle the entire earth like Satan in the time of Job, and you will not find the peace and tranquility of conscience you will in the humility of simply obeying your Prelate, and in the exact observance of the Law.

Woe unto them who are first to break the Law or Rule of the Prelate, for they sin without example, and they precipitate the scandal of others! Adam's sin did not damage him so much for being a serious one as it did because it was the first one.

The Legislator, although he is not subject to the penalty of the Law, is not exempt from guilt; for it is not a greater deformity for the head to disagree with its members than for the members to disagree with their head.

Predestined Pilgrim and His Brother Reprobate

PART IV

CHAPTER I

Of what happened to Reprobate after he left Bethoron.

At a giant's pace, having forgotten God and the good example of his brother
Predestined, Reprobate made his way toward Babylon as though he were headed
straight for Jerusalem. He left Bethoron where he had been all this time living
at ease, willfully, disobediently, whimsically, roughly, and obstinately. By and by,
he became an Atheist, or disciple of Epicurus. But who would leave a land that,
by interpretation, is the House of License, where Appetite and Fantasy governed,
and where Appetite carried out anything that came to the imagination of Fantasy?

The passport that the City Governors gave to Reprobate was issued according to the custom of Bethoron, and was very desirable in Babylon. It read: "*In-
imicus Crucis Christi, cujus finis interitus, cujus Deus venter est.*" That is, this man is
very much an enemy of the Cross of Christ, and who has no other vision in what
he does than that of Death, and no other God than his belly. With this document tucked into his breast pocket, or heart, he resolved to begin his journey.
But . . . by what route? Ah, through the delicious lands this side of Jordan, that
the children of Gad and Manassas chose for their inheritance because the land
provided fertile pastures for their animals, they having forgotten the other part
beyond Jordan that flowed with milk and butter. So it was that through these
lands Reprobate made his way, and he found rest in the land of Edom, which, interpreted, is deliciousness or delights, because, according to the etymology of its
name, it seemed to meet the needs of his pleasure. Edom, or the City of Delight,
was governed at this time by a very effeminate man named Pleasure, married to a
delicate and sensitive woman named Deliciousness, whose Palace was managed
by a stout young man who was its majordomo or Chief Guardian. I-Like-Me-
A-Lot was his name—a man pleasant enough at first sight, and much loved by
their lordships.

Edom's dwellers were impressively voluptuous, which is why the merchants
sold nothing but silks, fine linens, candies, perfumes, and tobacco. It was a pity
to watch these miserables take coins from their mouths and put them up their
nose, for many went without food so they could buy their snuff. I saw many keep
huge accounts for flowers, tobacco, and perfumes; yet they had no money to give
a coin to the poor, or to buy bread for the hungry. Others, who were deeply in
debt, spent much coin on fine clothing, gloves, and wigs. Even more horrific was
to see the parents spoiled and their children famished, their pages finely dressed
and their sons threadbare, their mistresses clothed and their daughters naked,
their beds lined with pillows and silken curtains while the Altars of God were
left destitute, lacking everything. This was the style in which Pleasure and Deliciousness governed through the offices of their Majordomo, I-Like-Me-A-Lot.
As soon as Reprobate presented his passport, he was received by Pleasure and

given a comfortable room much to his liking by order of I-Like-Me-A-Lot. As he had come from Bethoron, used to having everything his way, the Majordomo sought to please him in every way, removing from his presence anything that might be seen as a bother. In a few short days he had become voluptuous, ignominious, pleasureful, and truly an enemy of the Cross of Christ.

Here he became ill from a disease common to the land called Spoil, and from this illness sprang many complications like Laziness, Carelessness, Lassitude, and Halfheartedness. He quickly lost his appetite for the remedies which can cure Spoil—Penance and Rigor, and when they spoke about them to him, his countenance altered noticeably. But, even sick with Spoil as he was, a number of children were born to him here in Edom. They looked very much like him, for he had fathered Delight, Pleasure, Pastime, Rest, and finally two others: Deliciousness and Recreation. He lived with them all in the City of Delight, like another Heliogabalus of Rome, or truly like the glutton in the gospel.

When the ears of his brother, Predestined, heard this news, they say he exclaimed, "Oh, foolish brother, how erroneously you travel! And how your appetite has deceived you! God made the deliciousness of this world for us to sample, not to wallow in—to be a means, not to be the end of our existence. That is why it is customary to eat honey with the point of your finger, and not by the handful, as a Gentile put it very well. You ought to consider the delights of this world as things that evanesce, not as things that come—fleeting things, not permanent ones. That is why Gideon's soldiers drank water at the river with only one hand, and not lying flat on the ground drinking to their soul's content, as did the soldiers that God condemned. Do you not remember
the glutton in the gospel who was enticing his spiritual soul with carnal
delicacies the night that demons carried him off to Hell? Do you
forget the worldly miser who went from the worldly delights
and precious wines of this life to his fiery rewards
in the eternal one? Open your eyes, oh brother of
mine deceived, and consider that traveling
through Edom as they did, you will
end up in Babylon just
as they did."

༄

CHAPTER II

How Predestined left Bethany and what happened to him along the way.

These were the steps taken by Reprobate after he left Bethoron; different ones were those of Predestined after he left Bethany. He traveled, or better said, he ran like another David along the Way of the Commandment of God after the Lord in His mercy had enlarged his heart for that purpose. He walked along meditating on his Commandments that he dearly loved, fingering the promissory gathering of dictates that Observance and that Holy Virgin, Obedience, had given him in Bethany. After traveling what seemed to him a great distance, he found himself at the head of two rocky, harsh-looking roads. Bewildered by the question of which was the true road to Jerusalem, he said a prayer in his heart, asking God to show the way, repeating David's words: *"Vias tuas demonstra mihi, & semitas tuas edoce me."*[48]

Absorbed in his perplexity, he was approached by an extremely kind and resplendent young man who looked like an Angel from Heaven. He carried a Book in one hand; over the book was a ruler and a compass. In the other hand was a Cross, and with the light that emanated from him, he brightened both of those roads in such a way that all the tripping places and ditches that might be encountered could be seen. Predestined was overjoyed to see such a Seraph, particularly after putting to the test the truth, sincerity, and exactness of his words. He asked the visitor his name and who he was. The visitor told him that his name was Evangel and that he was the Chief Cosmographer of the ways of God, where the Cross was the landmark of them all; the Book contained the counsels of the Gospel; the ruler and the compass were the measuring sticks according to each one; and of those two roads one was called Penitence, and would lead to Capernaum, which, interpreted, is Field of Penance; the other was Counsels, and would lead directly to Bethel, or House of God. Although both roads look somber and rocky, with the light that Evangel emits they become much clearer and happier roads on which to travel.

"And if you, Pilgrim, had not followed the counsel of Obedience, who until now has guided you, know that you could not take one step in the Way of the Commandments without my counsel, without my light. All those who refused to be guided by the truth and sincerity with which I send off everyone, all those who averted their eyes from this landmark Cross which has distinguished the ways of the Lord, have erred and found themselves in Babylon, when they thought they were headed for Jerusalem."

Fearful of committing that same error, Predestined asked Evangel, "Which of these roads should I take?"

---

[48] "Show me Thy ways; teach my Thy paths."

"The Way of the Counsels," the Saint told him, "is the way of greater perfection; the Way of Penance is the one of greater need, because one can get to Jerusalem very well without going through Bethel, but you cannot go to Jerusalem without going through Capernaum."

What he meant was that without following the Counsels, one could obtain Salvation. But without Penance, there could be no Salvation once a person has sinned.

He added that the City of Bethel, since Perfection or Charity lived there, was built upon the two very high mountains of Incense and Myrrh. To reach it, one needed two dove's wings, that is, the innocent life that Predestined had not yet obtained, and for him to have to make that climb on foot might prove that he lacked enough spiritual strength, because of the falls he had taken along the Way of the Commandments of the Lord. He still had open wounds that he had received in his homeland Egypt. And they would not heal until he reached Capernaum, Field of Penitence, for only there could be found the remedies for such wounds and the Surgeons that know how to heal them. "Besides that," added Evangel, "if you choose to walk the Way of Penance — although rocky — after you become familiar with Capernaum, you will be much more disposed toward the Way of the Counsels going to Bethel, or Perfection, because it will teach you a shortcut, very short and sure, that leads there. And if you, Pilgrim, are still anxious to get to Jerusalem and follow the steps Christ took to get there, you must make Capernaum your dwelling place because Capernaum was a city so frequented by the Lord that it came to be known as the City of Christ."

∽

CHAPTER III

How Predestined traveled the Way of Penance.

Thus Predestined began his journey along the Way of Penance. No sooner had he begun his walk than he felt seriously ill, bothered by certain ailments that customarily beset beginners: Weakness, Repugnance, and Imagination. But he found a prescription from a great doctor named Bishop Augustine, who in Nazareth had taught him about such necessities. He found that it read, "*Non sufficit mores in melius immutare, nisi de his, quefacta sunt, Deo satisfacias per paenitentia dolorem*," which means: "It is not enough to change your life [for the better], if there has been no Penance for the past."

A little further down the road, he came to a raised berm called Difficulties-Along-The-Way which, when passed, led him up onto a very flat plain called Resolution. When he reached it, words cannot express how flat and easy the rest of the Way of Penance seemed to him. Before he reached the plain, or Resolution, the way seemed rough and craggy. Suddenly he understood by his own experience that the Way of Penance was not as difficult as it appeared: it was all about Resolution.

The Way of Penance, once the plateau was reached, was so brief that in no time Predestined found himself at the gates of the Holy City of Capernaum, or Field of Penitence. After entering, without the difficulties that he had first imagined, the first thing he did was go present his passport to the Chief Guard of the city, called Repentance of the Past. The Holy City of Penitence was governed at that time, as it always had been, by a noble servant named Holy Discipline and his wife, a severe matron, called Just Penance. Before Predestined went to kiss the governors' hands, as he had arrived tired and thirsty from his journey, Repentance of the Past took him to a spring or fountain in the City, which some call Tears and others call Crying, so that he could drink his fill and refresh himself. The design of this fountain was marvelous. It had two spouts, called Eyes: through one ran a bitter water called Sinner's Tears; through the other came water so sweet the Angels of Heaven drank from it, and even God himself enjoyed watching it. That is why Saint Bernard called it not water, but Wine of Angels. This water sprang from a rock, or heart, hidden in the depths of an earth called our flesh, drawn through a secret channel called Pain or Sentiment. Mysterious was the secret of this fountain, and marvelous was the virtue of its water.

The secret that made this fountain run was a spring or spigot of seven faces called Knowledge. On each face was written the letter P, and around the spigot were the words from Deuteronomy, "*Coram Domino Septies,*"[49] for all those who wished to make that water run had to walk around that spigot seven times. That is, they had to consider before God the mysteries of those P's. At the first P, they had to consider Peccation committed; at the second, the Punishment that for it they deserved; at the third, the Prize eternal lost for that peccation; at the fourth, the Privation of grace that peccation causes; at the fifth, the Passion of Christ which occasioned peccation; at the sixth, the Power of God to punish him who commits even peccadillos; at the seventh, the Power of God to Pardon him who cries. All those who know this circular path, or he who knows how to consider these seven precepts before God will, without doubt, make this water flow.

Who can give a worthy explanation of all the virtues of this water? In the opinion of Saint Ambrose, this water has the virtue of cleansing the soul from the stain of guilt. Saint Jerome thought that its virtue could soften the heart of God and tie the hands of Divine Justice. Saint Bernard's idea was that its virtue gladdens Angels and frightens demons, and in the opinion of many Church Fathers, this water's virtue heals all the ailments of the soul.

$\sim$

---

[49] "Seven times before the Lord."

CHAPTER IV

How Predestined visited the Palace of Confession, Contrition, and Satisfaction.

After drinking deeply from this fountain, and crying for his sins, Predestined was anxious to visit the governors of the city, Holy Discipline and Just Penance, in their own palace because, as Saint Gregory said, one of the main virtues of that water was to move the heart to penance and discipline. But the Chief Guard of the City, Repentance of the Past, who at this point was guiding Predestined, told him resolutely that it was impossible to kiss the hand or see the house of their lordships without first speaking with three ladies, sisters of theirs, who lived in a certain Palace — secret and hidden — called Sacrament. United in a triple harmony, their names were Contrition, Confession, and Satisfaction.

They both went in (for without Repentance one cannot enter that abode), and the first thing that Repentance showed Predestined was a secluded cubicle where there was a very correct and diligent old man near a table on which there were two books, an inkwell, a pen, a lighted candle, and an Image of Christ Crucified. The cubicle was called Mechanism; the old man, Examination; the table, Remembrance; the candle, Conscience; the pen, Memory; the inkwell, Offense; the books — one a short account of Predestined's life, the other a digest of the all the Laws and Commandments of God. Predestined's guide wanted to show him that, prior to Confession, he needed to approach the Mechanism with exactness. For the examination to be good, it needed to be done by checking his conscience against the precepts, remembering all that in which he was delinquent for which he went to Confession. All must be done before the True Judge of our consciences, who is Christ.

From this cubicle or mechanism, they moved to an inner chamber; it was a bit darker, as though to mirror the sentiment of a beautiful, honest virgin they saw there. She was dressed in mourning, without rouge or adornment, and she was kneeling at the feet of a crucifix: she was a Magdalene bathed in tears. With one hand she beat her breast with a stone. The other was tied to the hand of Christ, whose eyes and mouth emitted a ray of light that penetrated her heart, on which was written, *"Tibi soli peccavi,"* [50] and under her feet was a globe of the world with the word *"Omnia."* [51]

Predestined easily understood that virgin to be Contrition, who must precede Confession. To be dressed for mourning implied the sentiment of having offended God. Her crying and beating her breast with the stone, called Pain, denotes that our Pain should come from our heart and not just from our mouth. The globe of the world underfoot bearing the word *"Omnia"* signifies that our feelings

---

[50] "To thee only have I sinned."
[51] "Everything."

should be for all things and that it should be for offences against God. And that is why her heart shows the words "*Tibi soli peccavi.*" The ray of light and the hand tied to that of Christ means for the one who truly repents, the Lord will not hold back His light nor His favor.

"And if you, Pilgrim (added his guide) wish to serve and love this virgin, that is, if you wish to have contrition for your sins, kneel with her at the feet of Christ, crucified for you, with your eyes fixed upon that Image, and consider whom you offend with your guilt—a Lord who, to save you, did not hesitate to shed His Blood and give His life for you upon a cross."

From this chamber they moved to a more secret one, where they saw a Priest sitting, who had some keys in his right hand. Under his left one he had a book, a staff, and a medicine chest. On his mouth there was a padlock and a veil over his eyes; only his ears were attentive and unimpeded. At the feet of this Priest there knelt a virgin dressed in white; she seemed simple, sincere, and true. Exposed were her face and breast, from which she took her own heart and offered it to the Priest. Predestined understood well the significance of all this: the Priest was Confessor; the Virgin, Confession. Repentance told him what the other articles meant: "The key in the Priest's hand signifies his power to open and close consciences; the staff, the book, and the medicines represent the three offices of Confessor, Judge, and Doctor; the padlock denotes his confidentiality; the eyes covered and the ears sharp means the Confessor must not regard the person who confesses, but the sin he hears. The simple, sincere, and true Virgin at his feet shows the nature of the good confession: simple, without exordium and useless preambles; sincere, without the pretense of doubtful opinions; true, without the vices of false answers. Having her face and breast exposed denotes that the Confession must be clear, without disguise, and that the penitent must disclose his whole heart to the Confessor, putting into his hands all of his conscience. That is what is meant by the Virgin's giving her heart to the Priest."

There was one more room to visit. When they entered it, they saw a woman dressed in a rough cloth like that of a hair shirt, occupied in a thousand difficult chores. The Pilgrim wondered why such a noble woman would be engaged in such humble and severe ministrations. His guide told him that the woman's name was Satisfaction. She follows Confession, and her ministrations are works of Penance, or satisfaction, and, in order to be so, they must be performed personally and not by others, when they are imposed by the Confessor.

And because human fragility is so great, and even lesser our ability to fully satisfy God, Satisfaction gave to Predestined an exact copy of the key that Christ gave to Saint Peter, with which to open a huge chest that contained a great treasure called the Treasure of the Church, from which he could take a note, or credit, called a Bull, which when presented to any merchant or Minister of the

Church, would yield a coin of precious gold, called Indulgence, with which he would be able to pay God liberally for his debts.

CHAPTER V

Of the rare examples that Predestined saw in the Palace of Confession,
Contrition, & Satisfaction.

In the first chamber, where the Holy Virgin of Contrition lived, Predestined saw the memories of those Pilgrim sinners who, in this life, gave us rare examples of contrition. The Royal Prophet David was shown at the feet of the Prophet Nathan, and the Magdalene was at Christ's. David was repeating the psalm Miserere; the Magdalene was washing Christ's feet and drying them with the hair on her head. He saw the two soldiers mentioned by John the Elder who died suddenly, overcome by the Contrition that brought them Salvation. He saw the sinful public woman, moved to Contrition by the words of Saint Vicente Ferreira, who died from pain and flew to heaven at that very spot. He saw the Paris student who, because of the vehemence of his Contrition, was unable to tell his sins to his Confessor, writing them instead on paper only to find that they became erased. He saw the Innkeeper freed by his Contrition from Demons who had snatched him into the air. He saw the young man from Brabant of depraved character who was thrown into the sea for the obstinacy of his sin; as he was drowning, he made an Act of Contrition and was saved. He saw a faithful painting of a scene beheld by his own eyes: an Evangelist was preaching to a great sinner. The sinner was wrapped in iron chains. Moved by the words of the Preacher, he shed a single tear that fell upon the chains and undid them all.

Among these contrite Predestineds, he saw many Reprobates who had been condemned for lack of true Contrition. They had passed on from this life as confessed persons, and with the other Church Sacraments, like the clergyman from Paris, mentioned by Cesario, and the Parisian Doctor, by whose posthumous voice, acknowledging his own condemnation, Saint Bruno and his companions were converted.

Predestined saw in the second room, where the Holy Virgin Confession lived, those rare scenes of Confession told in his book by Father Christopher da Veiga of the Company of Jesus, where Pilgrim was saddened by the unfortunate case of the Princess of England, daughter of King Hugobert, who was condemned by her imprudent Confessor. He saw many young virgins surrounded by iron chains amidst the flames of Hell, condemned because they had hidden their sins from their confessors, in spite of the many other holy works they had performed. He saw many who let too much time pass between confessions and could not confess well, and others whose frequent confessions brought them final, saving grace.

In the third chamber lived the Holy Virgin Satisfaction. Here he saw and marveled at the extraordinary and disciplined penances that other Predestined Pilgrims had undertaken in this life to satisfy their guilt. He saw Saint Simeon the Stylite, who spent thirty years in the sun and rain on top of a pillar, dressed in a cilice and iron chains. He saw Saint James, the hermit who lived in a sepulcher and innumerable other hermits crying in their desert caves. He saw Saint Eusebius—his neck chained in such a way on earth that he was unable to look heavenward for forty straight years just because he had let his curious eyes wander upward during a spiritual reading at church. He saw Emperor Otto, who had priests whip him for an entire day. He saw Saint John Guarino satisfying the demands of his sins by condemning himself to seven years of crawling through fields, eating weeds. There were infinite other examples that I do not mention.

Predestined read here the rigorous penances pointed out to sinners in the sacred canons of old. For a homicide, a sentence of seven years; for a sin against Chastity, four forty-day quarantines; for adultery, a five-year fast of bread and water, barefoot; and other notable rigors.

But the one that seemed most horrific to Predestined and served to deter any inclination toward halfheartedness was the Monastery of Penitents that anciently hosted the first Christians. There he saw Saint John Climacus with his own eyes. He saw some standing, crying all night long; others whose hands were chained behind their backs, their heads bowed, uttering nothing but the howls of lions; others, sitting on the ground with their heads between their knees, were dressed in the cilice and covered in ashes; others, sighing, beat upon their breasts; others looked like men of bronze, impervious to all the inclemencies of weather. No laughter or joy was heard or felt—only sobs and sighs. Made all contrite by the sight of these penitent saints, Predestined, through the repentance he felt in his heart for his sins, determined not only to make a full confession, but to fully satisfy its demands as well.

〜

CHAPTER VI

Predestined visits the Palace of Holy Discipline and Just Penance.

Now knowledgeable about the three Holy Sisters—Contrition, Confession, and Satisfaction—Predestined thought it was time to kiss the hand of the governors of Capernaum, Holy Discipline and Just Penance. He traveled along the Royal Highway of the Holy Cross in the company of Repentance of the Past, his constant Guide, Teacher, and Support on that road. Without the slightest resistance, he entered a very sumptuous room in which there were all kinds of people of every stripe and condition: Popes, Kings, Princes, Men of the Cloth, Lords, and slaves. Among them he recognized many Predestined Pilgrims who, after having lived for years in that City of Capernaum, with Holy Discipline and Just Penance, were today already resting in Jerusalem: our First Parents, David, Saint Peter, the Holy Magdalene, Saint Matthew, and countless others. "Oh, Blessed Penance," Pilgrim exclaimed, "who opens Heaven's Gate to the sinner! Necessary and useful is your company to those who have sinned. Through you the sinner is justified, and through you the innocent are made more holy."

Resolutely he began to ascend a very steep staircase called Difficulty, or Repugnance of the Flesh, and easily found his way to the chambers of Holy Discipline and Just Penance. Repentance saw that Predestined was amazed at how easily he had gained the top of so steep a set of stairs, and told him that in her company an ascent was always easy.

"Those that dare not try to climb, or falter on their way, have not begun their ascent with true Repentance of the Past, but with my brother, Fear of Punishment. For those possessed of a heartfelt repentance of their guilt, easily resolve their penance.

"Tell me, Pilgrim," urged Repentance, "of the two who sinned, David and Saul—both having repented—why did only David resolve to do penance, but not Saul—unless David's repentance was heartfelt while Saul's was not? Since both Judas and Peter were unfaithful to Christ, their Master, what is the reason that only Peter did penance? Well, Pilgrim, that is the reason that some climb the stairway easily, and others do not; some climb it with me, others with my brother. That is, some resolve to do penance with true repentance of the past, while others do so only with fear of punishment."

Finally, Predestined was able to look upon the faces of Holy Discipline and Just Penance. The four walls of their room were ornately decorated with paintings portraying those who in this life have left us rare examples of penance. Each wall held a cross so that no matter what your vantage point was, a cross would always be before your eyes. They asked Predestined what he sought in their house.

"To live with Holy Discipline," he said. "To do just penance for my sins and thereby become a citizen of Capernaum, or Field of Penitence, for only in this way can I find my way directly to Jerusalem, which, I hope, will be my final destination."

"You have been well instructed, Pilgrim," they answered. "And if you wish to live with us and be a dweller in this city, you must live the way we live, dress the way we dress, and eat what we eat. Our life is an asperous one: abstinence is our food, and a hair shirt is what we wear. What is left of our time we spend in prayer; what is left of or substance we give to the poor; our free time is given to mortification."

At the time their lordships were saying these words, Holy Discipline reminded them that at the top of the stairs called Difficulty of the Flesh, there was a sick old man named Moribund, leaning on two crutches called Old Age and

Infirmity, who had in mind to climb up to speak with their lordships, principally with Just Penance. Holy Discipline answered in the words of Saint Augustine: "*Paenitentia in sano, sana; in morte, mortua*": which means, "penance for the infirm exacerbates the infirmity, and the death of the dead. Penance at this hour, with these crutches, friend Moribund, is very difficult to find." As Discipline was saying this, he saw the old man die right there at the head of the stairs without getting to see the face of Penance.

"Oh, miserable us," exclaimed Predestined when this happened. "How mistaken we are to postpone penance until we are old, or until the hour of our death! People who repented when they were young found a place for penance, but among the aged few, if any, do."

"Do you suppose, Pilgrim," answered Just Penance, "that many have found me during this time or in this hour? I ask you with Saint Augustine, 'Can you die in this way, sure of Salvation?' "

"*Si securus hinc exiit, ego nescio*," quoted Predestined from the same doctor of the Church. [which means]"I do not know whether they pass on safely from this earth."

"Well, neither do I," said Penance. "*Paenitentiam dare possumus, securitatem autem non*, I was a witness to their repentance, but whether they were saved, I can neither confirm nor deny. *Non dico damnabitur, sed neque dico, liberabitur.*"

This reasoning left Predestined fearful. Shakily, he repeated the words of the apostle, "*Domine, quis salvus fiet?*"[52]

Seeing him in the clutches of trepidation, Repentance of the Past, who was always at his side, again quoted the same saint, "*Vis ergo a dubio liberari?*[53] *Tene certum, & demitte incertum,*[54] *Age paenitentiam, dum sanus es,*[55] *Si hoc ages, dico tibi, quod securus es.*"[56]

No sooner had he managed to shed fear from his heart, than he heard the loud shouts of a desperate man coming toward him: "*Ferat omnia Daemon!*" He looked to see who it might be, and he saw a handsome young man that Pope Saint Gregory tells about, who had led a ruinous life. Called to repentance, he answered disdainfully that at the hour of his death he would say three words, "*Miserere mei Deus,*"[11] and he would be saved. Then it happened that while he was crossing a bridge, his horse tripped and fell into the water. Tangled in the reins, he grew fearful that he could not free himself, shouting those desperate shouts. In the middle of his shouting, he died. He who presumed to save himself with three words, with three words was condemned.

∾

---

[52] "Lord, who can be saved?"
[53] "Would you like to have you doubt removed?"
[54] "Don't abandon certitude for doubt."
[55] "Do penance while you have health."
[56] "If you do this, I tell you, your salvation is secure."

CHAPTER VII

How Predestined was taught in the Palace by Holy Rigor and Just Penance.

From this example, Predestined became determined to do penance for his sins before old age made the job more difficult, and before death could deprive him of the possibility. He put everything in the hands of the governors of Capernaum, who delivered him to a close and sober relative of theirs named Temperance—the mother of numerous holy maidens who governed the whole Palace. They were Abstinence, Sobriety, Modesty, and Chastity. Through two servants—Mortification and Discretion—they organized all the affairs of Holy Discipline and Just Penance.

Predestined was awed by the vision of so circumspect a woman and her company of such Holy Maidens. Humbly, he inquired as to her condition and office, as well as those of her daughters, in the house of Holy Discipline and Just Penance. She answered in the following way: "Pilgrim, I am one of the Cardinal Virtues, and my office and condition is to temper the delights of taste as well as the tactfulness of arguments; that is why my name is Temperance. In the first of my three ages—what you call degrees—it is my calling to avoid all defects that might obfuscate or bring dishonor, like overeating and other disorders of the flesh. In my second age, I seek the company of those that may help me with this—my neighbors, or virtues, like Mortification of the Flesh (the guardian of the senses), Prayer, and Devotion. In the third age, it is my office to seek in the things of these senses only necessity and not pleasure; for me, there is no distinction between food and remedy.

"And in the house of Discipline and Penance, in order for their affairs to be arranged with the order and exactness that God wishes, I am helped by the ministrations of these four Virtues that you see here—all of them my daughters because they derive from me, and by me they are governed.

"To moderate the excesses of the first sense of Taste, who is an unruly slave in this house, I call upon my two oldest daughters, Abstinence and Sobriety. They, with the help of these two servants, Discretion and Mortification, moderate the excesses of the table and the bottle.

"Two other daughters—Modesty and Chastity—have been useful in moderating the disorders of the second sense, Touch, who is another rebellious slave. Employing the same two servants, they constrain the excesses of the bed and of fashion. In this way the affairs of this house of Holy Discipline and Just Penance are governed by me with Mortification of the Flesh and with the help of Discretion—always needed so that the virtue of penance does not degenerate into an excessive discipline, nor the fear of too excessive a discipline frustrate the virtue of Just Penance."

Predestined gladdened at the words of Temperance and became more and more resolute in his intention to follow the steps of Repentance of the Past. He said to Temperance, "I beseech you, Holy Maiden, for the love of that Lord you serve, to guide me in this house, so that I may serve these Lords, Holy Discipline and Just Penance, according to the laws of prudence, and remembering the laws of mortification as well."

She did so, delivering him to those Holy Virgins of hers so that, according to the rules of their laws, they could teach Predestined the necessary precepts.

First, Abstinence taught him to exchange eating for fasting, the sweet for the bitter, the delicious for the plain, and finally to seek in food not the delights of taste, but the necessity of nature. Her sister Sobriety taught him to sometimes leave all his wine with Mortification, and occasionally, with Discretion, to drink a little when demanded by a weak stomach, as Saint Paul counseled Timothy to do.

Similarly, he met with the two other holy maidens, Modesty and Chastity. Chastity, following the etymology of her name, taught Predestined to castigate his flesh with the hair shirt and with discipline, in order to repress stimulation and curb the venereal delights that are so contrary to Holy Discipline and Just Penance. This was done through the two servants, Discretion and Mortification. In order that Predestined more easily achieve that end, she availed herself of the holy dictates of her good sister Modesty, who taught him how to flee the soft comfort of the bed and to avoid the excesses in fashion, silks, fine linens, perfumes, tobacco, and other luxuries that offend Modesty and contradict Holy Discipline and Just Penance, whom Predestined desired to serve. All this was done by way of Discretion and Mortification, without whose help these Holy Maidens could have accomplished no virtuous thing in the house of Holy Discipline and Just Penance.

As this was happening—and, again, I don't know if by chance or by some design of Holy Discipline—an argumentative uproar ensued outside the Palace. It sounded like a fight or an uprising. Among the shouts were heard the words of Saint Paul: "*Caro concupiscit adversus spiritum, spiritus adversus carnem.*"[57] Come to find that it was two very committed combatants, a male and a female; the male was Willing Spirit, and quite robust, and the female was Weak Flesh. Flesh fought in such a way that it prevailed against the Spirit. She was so malicious that, although she drove the fight, she was the one who complained the most; whenever the Spirit resisted, Flesh filled the heavens with complaints and the earth with her yelling. Holy Discipline came to see what that rumpus was about, and by means of his ministers called Instruments of Penance and Mortification, he delivered Spirit to Reason, Predestined's companion; he seized Flesh by the belt with a chain of iron called Cilice. On her feet he clapped irons called Retreat. In her mouth he placed a bridle called Abstinence, and over the bridle, he put a lock called Fasting. He tied her hands with chords called Rigors, and in

---

[57] "The flesh lusteth against the Spirit, and the Spirit against the flesh."

this way he quieted them. Predestined became even more resolute about his good purposes.

∾

CHAPTER VIII

How Predestined entered the Valley of Afflictions and the Garden of Tribulations.

Predestined received the teaching of these two Holy Maidens with a humble heart, and continued steadfast in his desire to serve Holy Discipline and Just Penance. Even though in this he followed in the footsteps of Repentance, his body was not exempt from feeling the drain of discipline and the effects of penance. So, to buoy up his spirit and to give him some relief from so much penance and discipline, it seemed good to their lordships that the Pilgrim should go for a walk through the field of Capernaum, or Penance, perhaps to a valley called Afflictions or to a garden called Tribulations. He left quite excitedly in the company of Repentance of the Past, for without his guidance, he could neither have found his way nor endured his walk. He entered, thinking to find relief, but found only pain and tribulations. As soon as he stepped inside the garden, he found not flowers, but that everything was thorns, weeds, and scrub oak. These were called Tribulations. At every step, he was caught by thorns and brush. Instead of birds that usually brighten a forest atmosphere, he found the air full of wild mosquitos called Insults, Injuries, Affronts, and Murmurings, biting him all over and greatly afflicting him.

In place of healthful plants, there were poisonous weeds called Sickness, Ailments, and Infirmities, that bothered him immensely. In place of crystal-clear brooks that normally water and gladden a forest, he found turbid, bitter waters called Anguish and Afflictions. In sum, everything was contrary to other gardens and orchards that he knew.

Finding himself in a garden of such horror, first pricked by thorns, then bothered by mosquitos — on one hand, at risk among poisonous weeds, on the other, tormented by bitter waters — and seeing that instead of comfort, he was met with tribulations, he exclaimed, "I abjure such a garden! This is relief from so much discipline?"

To these words Repentance answered with some severity, "Quiet, Pilgrim, do not say such things. Do you not know that in my company Predestineds see thorns as flowers, mosquitoes as nightingales, poison as medicine, and bitter water as honeycomb? Do you not know that to him who repents in his heart and who desires to do just penance for his sins, tribulations are comfort, curses are prayers, bitterness is sweetness, and discomfort is recreation? Do you not know that God normally sends his Predestineds discomfort for recreation, work for alleviation, and castigation for consolation? Do you not know that those whom God loves He chastens, but him who is not a son, He does not punish? Do you not know that in order for a Predestined to enter heaven, it must be with many tribulations? Do you not know, Pilgrim, that you are Predestined? If you want to enter Jerusalem, you must first pass this way."

Wrapped up in the logic of those arguments, he was startled to see a wolf suddenly break from that brush with a lamb in its teeth. The lamb cried out painfully, "Oh, poor me! How much better it would have been for me to have been a victim of God at the sacred hands of the Priest, than to die here in the jaws of the wolf—miserable and without glory!"

The situation was that the lamb had been ready to be sacrificed on the Altar at the hands of the Priest; escaping from those hands, the lamb ended up in the grasp of the wolf, who had taken it in his teeth, all ready to swallow it. Now the lamb was mewling its disgrace, considering how much better it would have been to die at the hands of the Priest—a sacrifice to God—than succumb in the grasp of the wolf's teeth. God wished to show Predestined how to make virtue of necessity. Since he could not in this life escape anguish and tribulations, it would be better to be sacrificed to God, suffer them well, with His love, and with true desire to satisfy the demands of his sins, than to be sacrificed to necessity, without any particular merit.

Predestined was now willing to accept tribulations that came his way, whether heaven sent or caused by malicious men, but what he could not understand was what Repentance meant when she said that, in her company, thorns would be flowers. His experience was that flowers refreshed and thorns bothered. In the clutches of this perplexity, he saw before him a handsome young man crowned with thorns, a cross on his back, and in his hands, feet, and side, the marks of five wounds. In one hand he carried a crown of roses, in the other was a crown of thorns. Speaking with Predestined, he said, "This crown of flowers in this life becomes one of thorns in the next, and this crown of thorns in this life converts to one of flowers in the next. That, Pilgrim, is what Repentance wanted to tell you. Now, you choose. Which is better for you, the crown of flowers or the crown of thorns?"

By the signs, Predestined knew very well that this man was Jesus of Nazareth. He threw himself at His feet and with tears in his eyes answered, "Oh, Jesu of Nazareth, my heart! How well You know that the crown of thorns is best for me in this life, in order that I might enjoy the crown of flowers in the next one. For you chose not the flowery crown in this life, but the one of thorns."

As he was saying this, he saw that angels quickly appeared and began to fashion many crowns from the thorns, and from the branches in that orchard they made crosses. With some agitation, Predestined asked the Lord the reason for those crosses and those crowns. His answer was that Predestined should choose the heaviest one of the crosses, and from the crowns of thorns, the sharpest one.

"And, Lord," Predestined answered, "How shall I carry the largest cross, it being so heavy and I being so weak? And how shall I support these sharpest thorns, being of fragile constitution, as I am?"

"With my help and in my company, you can do it easily. Take them and try."

So he took one, and he picked up the sharpest crown, because he saw that this was the will of the Lord. The cross was exceedingly heavy, and the crown was more than painful. But the Lord, perceiving his good desire and upright intention, gave him two holy virgins—daughters of His, Fortitude and Patience—and in their company, he joyfully continued on his way, following in the footsteps of Jesus of Nazareth, who, with his own cross and crown of thorns, led the way, always within Predestined's sight.

They arrived at a small chapel called Penance, where, when he changed the form of the cross on his back, he saw how it was that same Lord was crucified upon it with three hard, penetrating nails. At such a sight, compassion leapt within Predestined, and he dropped to his knees, eyes brimming with tears, and said these words:

"Oh, eternal good of our souls! Oh, most patient Jesu! Who can complain of one's own problems seeing You on this cross? Who will not willingly take up his own cross seeing You nailed to yours? Who will not support the thorns of their own tribulations, seeing You crowned in thorns? If an innocent man can suffer this, what does the sinner deserve? If You suffer such cruel punishment for my sins, how can I not do penance for my own?"

Predestined uttered these and other words at the feet of Christ Crucified, and in this contemplation he spent many hours in that little chapel in the presence of the Holy Maidens, Fortitude and Patience.

CHAPTER IX

Of what happened to Predestined in the Chapel of Patience.

In order to confirm Predestined's conformity to the will of the Lord and to make sure that he could satisfy the demands of his sins in a worthy fashion, the Holy Virgins kept him in that Chapel of Patience for several days, so that he could meditate on the stations of the Passion of the Lord, which were devoutly copied there.

At the first station in the orchard, where the Lord was amidst the representations of His torments, sweating drops of blood, Fortitude pulled his heart from his breast, and, bathing it in that precious sweat, he wrote upon it the words, *"Non mea, sed tua voluntas fiat."*[58]

---

[58] "Not my will, but thine be done."

At the second station of the prison, Fortitude bound Predestined's heart tightly with bands of the Lord and sculpted on it the words of the Holy Spouse, "*Trahe me post te curremos.*"[59] At the third station, the whips, the two Holy Sisters, Fortitude and Patience, took up the scourges of the Lord and gave Predestined's heart many stripes until they saw written thereon the words of Saint Paul: "*Flagellat omnem filium, quem recipit.*"[60] They arrived at the fourth station—the coronation—where Patience encircled Predestined's heart with harsh and penetrating thorns, writing on it with the Lord's reed the words of Holy Job: "*Esse subsentibus delicias computabo.*"[61] The sight of the forlorn image of Ecce Homo impressed on his heart the words of the Pharisees: "*Tolle, tolle, crucifige eum,*"[62] meaning to Predestined that he should take his heart and crucify it with Christ through compassion, to be in closer conformity with the cross.

When they arrived at the sixth station of the cross of the Lord with the cross on his back, the Holy Sisters took Predestined's heart and left impressed upon it the sign of the Holy Cross. Below it they wrote the words of the Beloved: "*Ut signaculuum super cor tuum.*"[63] That is, you shall always hold a great love for the Cross of Christ and be content with the labors and tribulations of life.

Finally, they arrived at the seventh and last station of Christ crucified. They stretched forth Predestined's heart toward the cross and drove into it the very nails with which Christ himself had been crucified. Fortitude took the lance that had pierced the Lord's side, and Patience took the reed on which he had been offered vinegar, and they wrote the words of the Apostle: "*Christo confixus sum cruci,*"[64] along with these words of the same Apostle: "*Ego enim stigmata Domini mei in corpore meo porto.*"[65]

In this way Predestined's heart was rendered so marvelous, so resonant with the Cross, so committed to his good purposes of suffering and satisfying the demands of sin, that all the labors and tribulations of this life seemed bland in the face of such an example and in the company of such holy virgins. But he thought it now time to proceed on his journey, and he went to seek the blessing of their lordships, Holy Discipline and Just Penance, and receive from their hand the sign sealed with the following dictates.

∿

---

[59] "Bind me, Lord, with Your chords so that I might follow in Your footsteps along the Way of the Cross."

[60] "God whips all those whom he calls His sons."

[61] "I hold the thorns of my afflictions to be delicious compared to the thorns of my Lord Jesu."

[62] "Away with Him: Away with him: Crucify Him."

[63] "This seal shall you carry always in your heart."

[64] "I am crucified together with Christ."

[65] "I have had impressed upon me the wounds of my Lord Jesu."

CHAPTER X

Dictates that Predestined learned in the house of Holy Discipline and Just Penance.

If you cannot handle discipline in your youth, how can you in old age?

If in the passage of so many years of life you have not worked worthy penance, how can you during the space of one hour before death? If you are unable to work when you are healthy, how can you expect to do so in the hour of your infirmity? Saint Augustine was correct when he said: Penance done by the healthy is sound, but weak when done by the infirm, and dead when attempted in death. God promises pardon, but not another day, to the sinner: today's pardon is certain, but penance postponed until tomorrow is not. For this reason, God loves the call of the Dove, and He abhors the caw of the Crow. Because the Dove, lamenting, says *nunc*, now, and the Crow's harsh cry says *cras*, tomorrow, as Saint Augustine says.

He who is more ashamed of the penance than of the sin, feels his punishment more than his guilt and, above all, does not feel that he has offended God.

Nothing is of greater importance—nor at greater risk—than Salvation. Penance assures it; procrastination puts it at risk. It is a huge mistake, therefore, to leave until tomorrow as a possibility that which you could certainly do today.

We read in the Scriptures about many sinners who did penances worthy of their sins; only one, however, accomplished a true one at his death—and that was the good thief: only one, so that no one need despair; only one, so that no one may presume.

Doing penance is not as difficult as it seems: engaged in, it becomes easier; made habitual, it does no harm. For if a little poison every day will not kill, how can daily medicine be harmful? Indulging in delights is more harmful to the voluptuous than discipline is to penitents. For the penitent normally live longer with abstinence than do the indulgent with their luxuries.

Tell me: at the hour of your death, what would you give for one more day so you could discharge your sins? Would you not give everything you possess? Or that which you must leave? Well, why not take freely now that for which you would pay so dearly then?

Both luxuries and tribulations are equally brief in this life, and equally eternal in the next one. Tribulations correspond to luxuries in this life; luxuries correspond to tribulations in the eternities: therefore, it is of more value to suffer tribulations than to enjoy luxuries in this life.

A life of the cross and tribulations is, for all, the life of this life; often, greater crosses are experienced by the malicious with their luxuries than by good persons in their tribulations. And if you must, per force, depart this life crucified, it is better to go crucified with Dimas to Heaven, than with Gestas to Hell.

The sinner enters into two tacit agreements when he sins: first, he becomes a slave of the Devil when he resolves to sin; second, he forms a friendship with God when he repents. The first one is easy; the second one is difficult to obtain.

It is better to suffer an injury or tribulation patiently than to later undertake great penance and mortification willfully. For, without sin, I can forgo penance; but impatience I cannot indulge without guilt.

Ridiculous is he who wants to fight giants when he does not dare to fight with Pygmies. Foolish is he who challenges ferocious lions when he cannot abide weak mosquitoes. This is the state of those who desire to suffer the torments of martyrs when they cannot suffer an affront or an insignificant tribulation.

With God on my side, I need not fear all the tribulations and all the discomforts that life can send my way. What can my enemy take away from me that is worth more than God, whom no man can take from me? Worth more to me is the fruit of penance, which I get to keep, than all the honors, riches, and conveniences that I may lack. The Cross on the shoulder is carried in close proximity to the crown of the head; he who sheds the Cross from his shoulder also knocks the crown off his head. Become disillusioned: from the trunk of the cross that you cultivate in this life shall spring the laurels with which, in the next life, they shall plait your crown.

Who has suffered in this life more offences at the hands of men than he has favors at the hands of God? You count the instants in which God has blessed you, and they are all the instants of your life. Now count the hours or days when men have offended you, and you will discover how many more are the instants of blessing than the days of offence.

What does it matter if a medicine tastes bitter, if it is healthful, than very sweet? It does not matter that you feel the harshness of discipline when, for the health of your soul, it is better than the mildness of a favor.

Predestined Pilgrim and His Brother Reprobate

PART V

CHAPTER I

Of Reprobate's journey to the City of Babel.

Pleasures and delights are of such a condition in this life that, when desired, they torment, and if enjoyed, they become tedious. Predestined's brother, the Pilgrim Reprobate, experienced this truth firsthand. He who had so anxiously yearned to enter and live in Edom, City of Delights, had grown tired of luxuries and departed, to continue on his journey. His pilgrimage took him through the fields of Sanaar, near Babylon—the last leg of his journey, where he would find the City of Babel, which means confusion. For there almost all the dwellers in Edom end up—that is, all those who spend their lives in luxury, pleasure, and delight.

Since Reprobate left Edom, the City of Delights, so spoiled and indulged, there was no way that he would not eventually live in Babel, City of Confusion. He entered the city and was received the way those in Babel usually receive Edomites, or in the way Confusion customarily torments the voluptuous: with a thousand sadnesses, distastes, and disquietudes. At this time, two malicious and incestuous old men named Sin and Evil governed the city. They were enemies and haters of God, the worst thing there is in the world—worse even than all the Demons, and, in the opinion of many, of an infinite maliciousness. Reprobate presented his passport to them; in it were the words of Ezekiel: *"Ipse impius in iniquitate."*[66] And as such he was received and put up for the night in the very palace of the governors, Sin and Evil.

There lived in Babel, as though in their own city, those seven Harpies, or seven monsters, that are commonly called Capital Sins. When they learned of Reprobate's arrival, they sent him their customary greetings, the gifts and refreshments that they usually give. Pride sent him his daughter, Self-Esteem, and with her, Irritations, Retribution, and Insolence, and they brought to Reprobate much rancor, hate, and provocation. Avarice brought him her son, Love of Money, and with him Cares, Covetousness, and Ambitions, which caused Reprobate many injustices, thefts, and a frequently harrowed conscience. Lust sent him her sister, Sensuality, and with her a thousand occasions of detestable perversity that for Reprobate were the cause of many ailments, abuses, and destruction of property. Wrath sent her daughter, Vengeance, accompanied by much enmity, acrimony, and animus. They brought occasions to the Pilgrim of fights, jail time, and many life-threatening situations. Gluttony sent to him her maid, Overindulgence, and with her a thousand delicacies, desserts, and precious wines that were the cause of much ailment, hunger, and drunkenness for Reprobate. Envy sent her daughter, Suspicion, to him, along with a thousand Taunts, False Testimonies, and Rash Judgments; these were the cause in his life of much murmuring, evil-speaking, and estrangement. Sloth sent her firstborn son, Monotony of

---

[66] "This is a man, impious in his maliciousness."

Spiritual Things, and, with him, much half-heartedness, negligence, and slug-gishness that occasioned for Reprobate many broken rules, sins, and much ne-glect of the Divine Law.

Spoiled by so much attention and so many presents, Reprobate developed such a malignancy in his blood that he contracted the plague of the land, which was a listlessness of his senses and energy. Doctors call it Forgetfulness. He walked around like a Stupid—forgetful of God and of Salvation. Nor did he any longer feel the remorse of conscience that had once tormented him; now he swallowed horrendous sins and enormous evils like he was drinking a glass of water. For temporal things and things of his personal convenience, his senses were sharp and his energy was high—for he deeply felt the loss of any temporal thing—but, for the loss of any eternal thing, he felt nothing. He stayed in Babel in the company of Sin for so long that Reprobate was able to become the father of three more very rebellious daughters. His first was Hardness of Heart; the second was Blindness of Understanding; the third was Obstinate Will, and with them he lived a number of years in Babel, or City of Confusion. From them were born so many children that one can hardly count them. Miserable, blind, and obstinate, he lived a life with them in which he no longer seemed to be a man of reason, but rather one of those of whom the Prophet speaks: *"Sicut equus & mulus, quibus non est intellectus."*[67]

CHAPTER II

How Predestined departed Capernaum for the Holy City of Bethel.

After living for some years in the Holy City of Penance, and after spending days in the Valley of Anguish and the Garden of Tribulations, Predestined left in the company of Fortitude and Patience, intending to follow the way of the counsels in which he had been schooled by that great Cosmographer, Evangel. In the midst of that heavenly company, he began to follow the road which, in spite of being the right one, was not free from thieves and hunters that infested those environs. Not far into their trek, they were met by three well-known Babylonian thieves—World, the Devil, and Flesh—who, as soon as they glimpsed Predes-tined, made plans to rob him. They were particularly interested in his wife, Rea-son, and in his two children Good Desire and Upright Intention. But, urged by his companions Fortitude and Patience, he called out his dogs, Flight and Resis-tance, that he had brought from Nazareth. At the direction of Fortitude, he set Resistance upon the Devil and Flight upon Flesh.

---

[67] "Do not become like the horse and the mule, who have no understanding."

Finding themselves driven back from Predestined, these thieves shot arrows at him, called Temptations, which he deflected with a shield that Fortitude gave him, called Celestial Defense. He then pursued them with his friends Fortitude and Patience until they totally disappeared.

Continuing on his way, he met a number of hunters called Impediments to Perfection. Being from Babylonia or from those depraved cities through which Reprobate had passed, they caused Predestined some concern. These hunters were Self-Love, Love of Relatives, Love of Country, and Immoral Love; they were approached by dishonest-looking young women whose identity was Intimacy with Women, Intimacy with Princes, and Intimacy with Bad Men. All these hunters, although not thieves, were suspicious, and proved to be a constant harassment to those travelers found in the Way of Gospel Counsels. That is why they were known as Impediments to Perfection.

Bothered by this encounter, Predestined consulted with Fortitude about what they should do. She told him to consider them excommunicates and to neither greet them nor speak with them, avoiding conversation with them at all cost, as one does with excommunicates. For they are of such an inclination that if they did not pervert Predestined, they would likely pervert his wife, Reason, without whom he would lose his way. Thus instructed, Predestined made his way to the foothills of a high mountain commonly called Height of Perfection. On top of it sits the Holy City of Bethel, which means House of God, where they would certainly find the abode of Charity, or Perfection, whom Predestined desired to meet. The way up so high a mountain would have seemed difficult indeed had Charity, from where she was at the summit, not sent down to Predestined two marvelous wings with which he could not only travel, but fly upward to the Height of Perfection, in the company of the two holy sisters, Fortitude and Patience. The two wings were called Hate Evil and Love Good, more commonly known as Hatred of Sin and Ardent Desire for Perfection. With them Predestined easily ascended and entered the Holy City of Bethel, or House of God, where Charity governs. By his own experience, he learned that in order to reach the apex of perfection, the Pilgrim must come to know a visceral hate of sin and to nourish in his heart an ardent desire to reach perfection.

CHAPTER III

Of the Holy City of Bethel.

A look at the etymology of its name is enough to explain the excellence of this holy city. It means the House of God, and in it dwells and governs Charity. In it she lives and waits on God Himself, according to her divine and infallible promise. Here in this city, when it was still a desert, Jacob saw that mysterious ladder supported by God himself, and by which Angels from Heaven ascended and descended. Founded on this mystery, Bethel became from then on the mystical City of Perfection, for just as the spirits ascended by the steps of that ladder to the top where God was, even so in the House of God, which is the Church, Spiritual Men climb its steps along the way of spiritual life until they reach the height of perfection where God dwells.

The City of Bethel spreads out upon two hills that Sacred Soul called Mount Myrrh and Incense Hill when she said, "I shall go up to Mount Myrrh, and I shall climb Incense Hill," by which she meant the exercise of Prayer and Mortification; because on these two practices are extended the acts of all the virtues, even those of Charity, which is impossible to obtain without Prayer and Mortification.

All the tall buildings in the city are built high according to their foundations, Humility, Self-Deprecation, and Self-Abnegation: the deeper these foundations, the taller the building.

The city is divided into three boroughs, or three ways, called Purgative Way, Illuminative Way, and Unitive Way, because those are the three steps into which every spiritual life is divided. In the first borough live those called Initiates; in the second live the Proficient; and in the third live the Perfect. All receive nourishment from that tree of Nazareth called Spiritual Life, whose flowers are Desires, whose fruits are Works, and whose leaves are Intentions. There is this difference though: the Initiates partake of the first branch, called Purgative Life; the Proficient eat from the second branch, called Illuminative Life; and the Perfect eat from the third branch, called Unitive Life.

Charity, the maiden of most noble blood to be found in the House of God, governed all three of these boroughs because in her is found the essence of perfection. All of her citizens are called the Just, the Saints, or the Servants of God. But because perfection does not reside, as they say, in the mindset, but in acts, she keeps always at her side two sons, Love of God and Love of Neighbor, and that is why Christ, our all, said in the Gospel that everything was founded upon them.

This great Queen, who rules all the virtues by her own immense virtue, lives in three different palaces—one in each borough, one on each way—all at the same time, so that it might be understood how all three are states of perfection, even though each is in a state of more or less perfection, but no one is found there who is not partaking of the grace and friendship of God. The first Palace is called Clean Heart and is found in the borough or way called Purgative. The second is called Enlightened Heart and is on Illuminative Way, in that borough. The third is Perfect Heart or, as Christ called it, Optimum Heart, and is found on Unitive Way. In the first palace, Charity teaches the first doctrines of perfection to the Initiates. In the second she dictates lessons to the Proficient. And in the third, she teaches dictates of love to the Perfect.

But because great ladies do not usually govern personally over the ministrations of their houses, Charity had two saintly maidens, Prayer and Mortification, who, although of different blood, were so united as sisters with Charity that they could not be separated. Thus, it was impossible to find Prayer without Mortification, or Mortification without Prayer. So through these capable mistresses or teachers, all were governed, and all three of Charity's palaces were kept orderly. If it were not for the intermediary service of these maidens, it would be very difficult to talk with her ladyship, that is, to reach Perfection. As ancient Cosmographers say, the names of these two maidens are found on Mount Myrrh and Incense Hill, where the City of Bethel is situated, understanding that Myrrh means Mortification, and Incense means Prayer, according to that which the daughters of Zion discover in the happy soul: for among perfumes and aromas, those of Myrrh and Incense stand out.[68]

CHAPTER IV

Of the first borough of Bethel, and what happened there to Predestined.

Predestined was exceedingly happy to find himself in the Sacred City of Bethel, because he saw himself, like Jacob, not only in the House of God, but at Heaven's Gate, or the gate of Celestial Jerusalem, the object of his journey's quest. The two sisters, Prayer and Mortification, found lodging for him as an initiate in spiritual life in the first borough or way, called Purgative. It was there that they gave him his first instruction on perfection. First they told him how his meals must come from the first branch of that tree of Spiritual Life, called Purgative Way, and how he would now become a farmer in that borough. His time would be occupied in working, digging, and plowing the earth of his soul with the plow of Mortification, weeding out the thorns and noxious nettles of vice and bad inclinations, and how he would then irrigate — fertilizing with celestial dew and water by means of the holy exercise of Prayer.

Thus continued Predestined under the guidance of his instructors, these holy sisters; he perspired and worked at removing the thorns and weeds from his old vices. But just when in one part it looked like the earth of his heart was clean, up sprang weeds in another part, and more thorns troubled his earth. The more he tilled every day, the more noxiousness seemed to spring up. The two sisters explained that it was because he was just cutting out stalks and branches, and not getting at the root. "What does it matter, Pilgrim," they said, "that your sickle cuts the branch away if you leave the root in the soil? Will it not sprout up again?"

---

[68] Song of Solomon 3:6.

Predestined saw that this was so, and from then on he began to use the Plow of Mortification in such a way that cut deeply into the earth and uprooted the cause of that obnoxiousness, the roots themselves.

But the roots of certain weeds gave him more trouble than others—those that we call bad habits, or bad customs—and no matter how hard he worked, he seemed not be able to completely uproot them all, for they sprang up here and there. To remedy the matter, besides the plow that Mortification had lent him, Prayer gave him a beautiful instrument called a Particular Examination of Conscience, which he used three times a day and soon thereafter easily uprooted the roots of his bad customs and ruinous habits.

Predestined continued to work on the spiritual cultivation of his soul, and he no longer felt the old weeds of his previous sins and vices springing up, for he had removed their roots. From time to time, however, he did feel sprouting certain little useless plants called Bad Inclinations, and occasionally these plants actually bore tiny fruits called Venial Faults, or imperfections by another name. Although they are not poisonous, they are disagreeable and are offensive to Charity. Pilgrim examined the cause of this phenomenon and found that there was actually dirt in the spouts that carry the water that irrigates the soil of our heart and soul. Since the water had become polluted, so did the land, and soon enough these little plants began to emerge, resulting in these tiny fruits. The fountains must be kept clean so that only pure water will flow. These fountains are none other than the two driving components of our soul: Understanding and Will, whence all good and evil proceed. They both flow through two pipes called Sensitive Appetites. The last name of one is Irascible; the other is Concupiscible. They both flow through eleven little streams called Passions; Concupiscible has five, and Irascible has six. Concupiscible's streams are Love, Hate, Desire, Abomination, Delight, Enjoyment, and Sadness. Irascible's pipes are Hope, Desperation, Daring, Fear, Anger, and Indignation.

The first fountain of Understanding gets infected with a sticky moss called Bad Dictates. The second fountain, Will, succumbs to Bad Emotions. If our Understanding is contaminated with depraved dictates, or doctrines other than those of our profession—if Will becomes depraved by the disorderly affectations of our passions—how can our understanding square with truth, and how can our will follow what is good? For they are the formal objects of their moral operations.

"And what shall I do," Predestined asked his two Instructors, "to keep these fountains clean, so that the water that flows there is always pure?"

"The remedy," they answered, "you have at home. Turn this worry over to your wife, Reason, and to your children, Good Desire and Upright Intention; they know how to keep fountains clean and water pure. First, Reason, through your daughter Upright Intention, will assume the care of purifying or directing Understanding, making sure to have always in view the highest truth, which is God. Then, by way of Good Desire, she will be careful to keep Will in order, keeping in mind the highest good, which is God himself. When everything is governed by Reason together with Holy Desire and Upright Intention, only pure water will flow from this fountain. As a result, the earth of our heart and soul will remain clean. And if one of those little weeds called Inadvertencies begins to sprout, or one of those little fruits called *Actus primi*,[69] is seen, it will not be our fault, nor the fault of the gardener, but because the earth itself is bad and of poor quality."

Instructed about what his job would be, Predestined asked his teachers, Prayer and Mortification, where he should find his sustenance, for was it not a just thing that he who worked should also eat? They told him that as long as he lived on that first street, he should eat from the first branch of the Tree of Spiritual Life, called Purgative Life, whose leaves are called Intentions to Renew Your Life, whose flowers are Desires of Renewal, whose fruit is called Life Renewed, because all of it has the purgative virtue to clean and purge the heart of all four noxious humors that infect it: vices, sins, bad habits, and bad customs. First, Prayer taught him how to make a confection from the leaves and flowers that, besides their natural virtue of comforting the heart in preparation for its new life, has the additional virtue of purging dark spots or cataracts from the eyes. These are called Spiritual Darkness or, by another name, Lack of Light, and are purged so that the soul can begin to focus on four things very necessary for initiates: first, seeing the miserable state of their past life; second, seeing the present state of their distracted life; third, seeing the impediments that inhibit their conversion; fourth, seeing the means that can lead to a renewal.

She also taught him how to make a delicacy from the fruit that Heaven's Angels are very fond of: Sincere Conversion, which is the same as life renewal. In order for it to endure, it must be tempered with the salt of Mortification, conserved in the honey of Devotion—the latter through the doctrine of Prayer, the former by the precepts of Mortification.

But because this first branch has not only the virtue of nourishing spiritual life, but also the virtue of purging it of all faults and imperfections (and that is why they call it a Purgative Life), Charity sent Predestined to a very experienced doctor, whom they call Spiritual Father, to help in the application of the fruit, leaves, and flowers, according to his need. For this reason Predestined needed to disclose to him all of his ailments, pains, and infirmities, as well as his natural disposition and inclinations, so that the doctor would be in a position to cure him according to his needs in his present state. Charity was so impressed with this doctor that she normally confided to him the treatment of the health of all the pilgrims that lived in this borough, that is, the progress of all those beginning Spiritual Life.

---

[69] "First actuality."

In order to keep fresh and green not only this branch, but the whole Tree of Spiritual Life—particularly when it might show signs of wilting from the wind or from the heat of temptations—Charity, with mysterious providence, ordered that a cask of water from that fountain in Nazareth they call Sacrament of Penance be brought to this first borough, or Purgative Way. Because, if need be, watering the branch with that water would restore its freshness and pristine verdure. Predestined was quick to comply with this request, for he desired to reach perfection in the company of those Holy Virgins Prayer and Mortification, who never left his side and with whom he became very familiar.

CHAPTER V

Of the second borough of the City of Bethel.

After he had received the first instruction about perfection in the first borough, or Purgative Way, the two Holy Maidens Prayer and Mortification took Predestined to the next neighborhood or city way, called Illuminative Way, where he could be instructed in the principles of those already progressing in their spiritual life and were therefore called Proficient. "At first," they said, "your office will be that of a farmer, the same as you were before, but with this distinction: in the first borough you were principally concerned with plowing and clearing the earth of your soul; but in this second one you will be occupied in planting in that earth and cultivating the fruitful trees of all the virtues."

"For this," they continued, "you will divide the earth of your soul into four sections or corners, in order to plant in them the trees required by the good art of spiritual agriculture. In the first order, you should plant those trees or virtues that belong immediately to God. In the second, those that concern your superiors. In the third, those that belong to you. In the fourth, those that belong to others."

Those that belong to the first order or section are four plants: Faith, Hope, Charity, and Religion. Those of the second order are Observance and Obedience. Those of the third section are eight: Humility, Poverty, Chastity, Modesty, Temperance, Fortitude, Patience, and Meekness. Those of the fourth order are five: Justice, Friendship, Mercy, Fidelity, and Prudence. All these trees or virtues, besides their essences and properties, are found in three states which farmers call degrees. The first state or degree is that of beginners, the second is progression, the third is that of those who are perfect. Because, like the tree that first sprouts, then grows, and finally reaches a perfect fruit-bearing state, even so, any virtue in the soul first is born in grace, then it grows as it magnifies until it reaches its perfection. The method and art of planting these virtues are the same ones farmers use to plant trees. To plant a tree, the first thing a farmer does after the ground is cleared is to make the tree put roots down into the earth. To do that, the farmer gathers the earth, fertilizes it, and waters it with care until it sprouts and begins to push out its first buds. This is the first estate of the tree. The cultivator of the soul does the same thing with any virtue. First, he makes it sprout and root itself in humility, with a knowledge of our baseness until little leaves, or acts of that virtue, begin to emerge. This is a sure indication that the soul has reached its first degree. Like the tree in its first estate where the farmer insures that the plant takes root, the first thing to do is make sure with all certitude that the virtue thrives and takes root in the soul.

The second thing the farmer does to the tree is make it grow until it reaches its perfect state of bearing fruit. He does not allow it to bear fruit or even blossom before it reaches its proper state. To achieve this he makes sure to fertilize, prune, and water it so it will send down good roots, knowing that the tree will grow only in proportion to the depth of its roots. This is the second estate of a tree. The next thing that must be done in spiritual agriculture is to make sure that a virtue, first born in our soul, grows and enlarges—sending down strong roots—and does not linger on the surface of the earth. For it is a sure thing that all virtues in the soul are like the cypress in the field, whose branches grow as tall as its roots grow deep. This they commonly call the second degree, or Enlargement. The third way orchardmen regard their trees is to hope, after sufficient growth, that they reach a state of perfection. This state is recognized when the tree sends forth flowers and produces fruit. This is called the tree's third estate. Similarly, in spiritual agriculture, when the virtue in our soul swells to the extent that it not only flowers with good desires, but bears the fruit of good works as well, leading to generous and heroic acts, then we know that it has become a perfect virtue and this we call the third degree, or Perfection.

Now familiar with this work, Predestined asked his instructors where he should eat, since he would now be working in this borough. They answered, "From the second branch of the Tree of Spiritual Life, called Illuminative Life, for that is where the Proficient dine. On this branch you will find leaves, flowers, and fruit like on the others. The leaves are called Intention to Progress; the flowers are Desires for Greater Perfection; the fruit is Spiritual Enlargement." Charity had made such delicate dishes and desserts by her servants, Prayer and Mortification, that Predestined found them increasingly more palatable, both those seasoned by Mortification—somewhat salty and vinegary—and the ones produced by Prayer—sweeter and more gratifying—but the ones that they both cooked together, seasoned with the sourness of Mortification and the sweetness of Prayer, were the tastiest dishes. Day by day he grew spiritually fatter; day by day he acquired more strength which he willingly expended in the spiritual cultivation of his soul.

∿

CHAPTER VI

Of the first and second order of plants in this second borough of Bethel.

The plants that Predestined needed to cultivate in the second order or corner of the second borough are four, as we have mentioned: Faith, Hope, Charity, and Religion. All four belong exclusively to the Lord, who is God; for with them we immediately honor and respect God.

The first one, called Faith, is a divine, supernatural plant which God himself planted in the virgin earth of our soul on the day that it was cleansed from original sin and irrigated with the water of Baptism. The fruit of this tree is very similar to the fruit of the Tree of Knowledge where Adam sinned, because it has the virtue of opening the eyes of the Faithful Christian to know good from evil. That is, all that God has revealed without a shadow of a doubt or opinion. From its flowers a cordial is made, so mysterious that partaking of it inclines the heart to fearlessly affirm all the mysteries of our Religion.

The second plant, called Hope, is so completely green that it never wilts unless burned by the fires of desperation. Its fruit has the virtue to awaken the potential of our soul to the achievement of eternal Blessedness and to all other things which help lead thereto. From its flowers an admirable cordial is made which comforts the heart against urgent temptations, vanity, and the Devil's encroachment. It induces the heart toward an admiration of eternal things and an abhorrence of temporal ones.

The third one, called Charity, is the prettiest and most divine plant that God created. Its fruit compares in excellence to that of the Tree of Life that He planted in the middle of Terrestrial Paradise. For in the way the fruit of that one caused life in the body, this one enlivens the soul. Its fruit is so hot that it fires the heart and bowels of those who eat it, above all else, in the love of God. From its flowers is made a cordial that noticeably disposes one to love God and toward all other things that lead exclusively to that love. Moreover, those that know the virtue of this plant distill from its flowers, leaves, and fruit — that is, from works, desires, and intentions done with charity — a marvelous liqueur that has the virtue of uniting hearts and hands with the heart of God, making them conform as one in such a way that what one wants, the other wants too, without contradiction. This is the supreme virtue or quintessence of the plant.

The fourth tree, that they call Religion, is the most excellent of all the moral plants. In it, we give to God the honor due Him by reason of His divine, supreme being. It was planted from a cutting of the first tree, called Faith, because it is upon Faith that the virtue of Religion is grounded, and from it springs all adoration of the divine, and from it, all those servants of God who take upon themselves the name Religious derive their sustenance. When the flowers of this tree are applied to the heart, they predispose it to form a high concept and opinion of

Divine Being. Its fruits (which may be eaten only by the Faithful) are principally Adoration, Sacrifice, Sacrament, Oath, Prayer, and Devotion.

Two very similar trees are found in the second order; they spring from a branch of Charity with which we honor our superiors that act in the place of God. The first is Observance; the second Obedience. Observance has the virtue of inclining the heart toward reverencing persons in high office to whom we owe respect and veneration.

Obedience, which is one of the trees most pleasant to divine eyes—and from which Christ Himself ate all the time that He lived in this life—has the virtue of inclining our potential and our hearts toward the precepts of God and His Ministers that act in His place. As soon as it sprouts, it has the virtue of predisposing the heart toward prompt and joyful obedience. After it has grown a while, it inclines the Will toward an obedience both intuitive and pleasureful. When perfect, it impels the understanding to judge all precepts justly. The fruit of this tree is so important that without it one cannot endure life's journey along the road toward Eternity. For without it, one cannot take even one step in the Way of the Commandments of God.

Its worth is so great that Pope Saint Gregory said from it can be taken cuttings of all the other plants or virtues; and, in the opinion of Saint Ignatius, its branches surround and protect them all. As long as this plant flourishes in our soul, all the rest will be seen to flourish; for it is a sign that Charity, in which all are born, is green. But when she withers, all the rest dry up, because it is a sign that their root—Charity—has become dry.

CHAPTER VII

Of the third order of plants.

In this third order of plants are found those supernatural plants or virtues that belong to our spiritual growth or rest. The first of them is the one that seeks to be last in everything: Humility. Although highly esteemed and appreciated by God, it is a very low plant, with virtually no elevation. Its virtue moves the heart toward a knowledge of its vile self, and it is its own remedy for inclinations toward pride. It extends its long roots through those of the other plants and virtues. And the plant that is not rooted in or near this one is neither firmly planted nor secure. Since Humility tries to run its roots deeply under the earth, it follows that trees whose roots ramble along the surface of the earth cannot be rooted in Humility, and that is why with any puff of Pride they are ruined. This plant called Humility grounds itself on two very firm roots. The first is called Self-Knowledge; the second is Knowledge of God. From these spring two trunks, or branches, which constitute the whole tree. These are Humble Knowledge and Humble Affection.

The first belongs to Understanding; the second belongs to Will. The first branch is born from the first root, Self-Knowledge; the second branch grows from the second root, Knowledge of God. The first branch, or Humble Knowledge, has three effects that the cultivators of the spirit call degrees. As soon as it sprouts, it makes one know the defects that one has: this is its first degree. As it grows, it makes one familiar with not only his defects, but makes him believe in those he *presumes* to have: this is the second degree. When it is perfect, it makes him believe that he is the worst one of all, when truly he may be the best: this is the third degree. All this comes from knowing one's depravity; that is why we say that this first branch, or Humble Knowledge, is founded on the first root, called Self-Knowledge.

The second branch of this plant, or Humble Affection, has three other effects or degrees. Soon after it is born, it has the virtue of inclining the heart toward being in subjection to superiors: that is the first degree. After a while, it predisposes one to being subject to one's peers: this is the second degree. And when it is perfect, it inclines one to be in subjection to one's inferiors. This is the third degree of Humble Affection. All of this is born from the Knowledge of God and His excellence. This is why we say that this branch derives from the first root, called Knowledge of God. The flowers of this plant, or Humble Thoughts, adorn all the other plants. For all are set in Humility, and all are defined in its context. With these flowers alone, the humble heart is made. The fruits of this tree are the effects that holy humility causes in our souls; they are innumerable and cannot be counted. From this tree of Humility grows a branch called Poor in Spirit, much esteemed by Christ, the Supreme Orchardman, who was the first to plant it on the land. Its branches do not spread widely, nor is its foliage very abundant, for the Poor are content with very little. It has the virtue of quenching the thirst of covetousness; when eaten, it causes an aversion to riches, and tempers the fires of ambition.

This plant is supported by two roots called Admiration of Eternal Things and Aversion to Temporal Things. The first of these is rooted in Humility and the other in Temperance, so its flowers, or desires, have two marvelous effects in the heart: they cause loathing of money, and the love of its absence.

Its fruits are the effects it causes in the truly Poor of Spirit, which are many. The principal one is a peaceful soul and a stillness of conscience born in their disentanglement from the worldly things that so complicate the things of Heaven — so much so that from the very doctrine of Christ, the Supreme Orchardman, one surmises that whoever does not carry in his hand a branch from this tree will find it very difficult to enter His orchard, which is Paradise.

Near this tree is a plant of inestimable beauty because it appears to be a flower, all white in color, angelic in nature, called Chastity, and its virtue is to repress the stimulation of sensuality and to bridle the sexual passions. It is a very demanding plant; almost any breeze will be its undoing, and it is disgraced by the smallest speck of dirt. This is why nature or, better said, grace, has surrounded it with the branches of all other plants or with the acts of all the virtues, for all are necessary for its security. Still, it is not possible to guard it against the squalid flies of sordid thoughts that endeavor to suck the substance from it, or at least the dew from Heaven on which it feeds itself, grows, and on which it thrives.

When this plant is small, it generates in those who use it, a horror of all dishonesty; when it has grown, it inspires a love of all things pure; when it is perfect, it makes of those who partake of it, that is, those who keep it, Angels of God in the flesh. A flower blooms on this plant that among all others is most beautiful. It is called Virginity or, euphemistically, flower, of which they say the chaplet is made which crowns the Lamb of God. It is also the sign or glory of all the Spouses of Jesus Christ, and if it withers, it can by no means be brought to flower again. From this and the other flowers on this plant—Good Purposes and Chaste Thoughts—a liqueur is distilled that somehow purifies the heart and almost spiritualizes our flesh.

Similar in beauty, but very different in color, is another plant they call Modesty. Its flowers are red, and this is its sign: its exterior composition is marvelously well organized, symbolic of the interior virtue of its substance. For it is certain that, like the life and interior virtue of any plant, even so is its surface beauty and exterior form. And in this plant or virtue, more than in any other, its inner virtue is deduced from its exterior beauty.

Although all the plants in this orchard are very beautiful, this one is a credit and a beauty to them all, because its principal virtue is to arrange and beautify the exterior of its body so that it conforms exactly to the inner order and beauty of its soul. When it first sprouts, it has the virtue of communicating to those who possess this tree, a loathing of all disorderliness. As it matures, those who behold it are impelled to organize their exteriors in conformation with their inner soul. And when the tree reaches perfection, it orders all its powers in such a way that its acts—both hidden and observed—cause in the spirits of all around it a reverential awe or a reverent love of the modesty of Christ and the similar modesty of his Mother. The flowers of this plant are extremely fragrant, the most aromatic of all of them. This is why the Apostle called them the good balm of Christ. They persuade the heart to love the true, solid virtues and to abhor all fiction and hypocrisy. Its fruits are very healthful to the eyes and heart; they are called Good Name, Good Example, and Edification.

These last two plants, Modesty and Chastity, grow from the roots of a tree called Temperance, whose virtue is to moderate and harmonize the sense organs of taste and touch, reducing them to the constraints of Reason. Two branches grow there called Abstinence and Sobriety, of which the first moderates the overindulgence of eating, and the second, the disorders of drinking. When its flowers are applied to the heart, they affect both hunger and satiety, producing a hunger for insipidity and an aversion to celebratory libation, and in a marvelous way they comfort the heart to seek through eating only that which is necessary, not that which delights. Its fruits are those that Mortification has learned to gather and Penance has learned to temper, of which the most notable one is the fast. Near this plant are two other trees very similar in effect, but different in stature. One called Fortitude is as hard as steel; the other one, as soft as wax, is called Gentleness.

Fortitude has the virtue of fortifying the heart against the difficulties of Spiritual Life. When it is born, it excites the heart to flee all sin and, when perfect, to despise all fears — even of Death itself. The flowers or effects of this plant fortify the heart to suffer much adversity for the Glory of God, and its fruits are the victories over the most terrible of temptations.

The one called Gentleness has the virtue of deflecting the impetus of anger. The virtue of its flowers is to soften the heart, cure the tumors of anger, and repress the fervor of indignation. Its fruits are to give good for evil: peace, quietude, brotherly love, compassion, tranquility, and to be pleasing in its dealings.

Near these two trees is yet another similar one, even more necessary to spiritual life. They call it Patience. Its virtue is to suffer all adversity with constancy and to temper any sadness that might be conceived because of it. Initially, it expels from the heart all impatience or sadness; then, when grown, it enables one to tolerate adversity with joy, and in its perfect state, it inspires a hunger for adversity. Its flowers are a great boon to the heart in its infirmities and tribulations. Its fruits are proof of God, merit, and satisfaction.

~

CHAPTER VIII

Of the fourth order of plants.

In the fourth and last order of trees, or virtues, are found those plants that of their own accord bear fruit for others — at no loss to the orchardman of his principal fruit, which is his merit. In the foreground is a very symmetrical tree, whose branches, similar to those of a Palm, did not hang down more on one side than another, and whose branches could not be bent. Its fruit was also symmetrical in size and weight. Its roots would not grow in the ground of another. This plant signified the virtue of Justice, which is to give to all equally that which is theirs.

When it sprouts, if applied to the heart, it causes an aversion to the possessions of others. In its maturity, it affixes in the heart the commonplace: wish not for others what you would not wish for yourself. When perfect, it makes one put the rights of others before one's own. Its flowers make the heart generous, make it despise unjust interest, and make it an egalitarian heart. Its fruits are its acts — too many to be counted.

From the root of this plant grows a branch called Fidelity, whose virtue is to keep promises. A flower called Truth grows from it that cannot droop. It bears a fruit called Loyalty, which has within it a well-kept seed called Secret. This plant is highly sought after for its virtue of comforting noble and generous hearts.

Next is a handsome tree, one of the most pleasant and profitable in the orchard, called Fraternal Charity, also known by the name Friendship. It grows from the best branch and the best root of Charity of God herself. Its admirable virtue is to unite the hearts of those who find their love in Christ, and so it is known as Fraternal Union as well. Everything about this tree has the virtue to unify: leaves, flowers, fruits. That is, effects and thought: neither contemplating, nor doing any work offensive to the love owed one's neighbor; rather, empathizing with him in one's thought, desiring for him all good things in one's affection, and doing all possible good for him in one's works. From this tree grows a long branch named Mercy, under whose shade gather all the homeless poor. Its fruit is so valuable to divine eyes that it is bought at the cost of eternal glory. Its virtue is to cause compassion for the miserable, and its flowers incline the heart naturally toward piety.

This whole orchard or garden of the Holy City of Bethel is crowned by a handsome, mysterious tree, very similar to the Tree of the Knowledge of Good and Evil in Paradise. It is called Celestial Prudence to distinguish it from another, similar tree in the world called Carnal Prudence. Its virtue is to open the eyes to know the good from the bad and to influence the heart to choose prudently in order to obtain Blessedness. It extends its branches and roots around all the plants in the orchard, for none of them, without Prudence, has the virtue to produce its proper fruit. It is fed by its principal root, Light of Faith, which, in turn, sends out four other roots called Experience, Perspicacity, Conscience, and Docility. Its trunk is Counsel; its branches, Purity of Intention; its flowers, Constancy, Diligence, and Efficacy. Its fruits are Election, Execution, Determination of Time, and Determination of Mode.

CHAPTER IX

Of the third borough of the Holy City of Bethel.

Seeing so many beautiful and mysterious plants amazed Predestined. After learning from the two Saintly Sisters, Prayer and Mortification, the precepts of agriculture and instructions for cultivation, the intense desire of his heart was to visit the third borough of the city they call the Perfect or Unitive Way, because from its name he deduced that in it were many perfect things to admire.

Charity read Predestined's heart and lovingly reprimanded him, saying this was not the best reason to visit that neighborhood, but perhaps he might search there for the perfection of Charity, known also by the name of Perfect Sanctity, and look as well to unite himself with God through contemplation. Because this is the reason that the place is called Unitive Avenue, and those who live there, the Perfect.

These things seemed to Predestined to be of a higher spiritual plane, and since Charity was already in a state of perfection, he felt confident to ask her, "What is Sanctity? And what is Contemplation?" to see if he might find within himself the capacity to achieve such sublime states.

"You should know, Pilgrim," answered the Holy Virgin, "that in the general sense, Sanctity is nothing other than justice and moral goodness as they proceed from the grace and charity of God. Included in it are essentially two things: the first is grace, and the second is propriety of behavior. In this sense, those who enjoy this state of grace are called the Just and the Saints. Although they are very well behaved, they have, nevertheless, not yet reached the state of sanctity to which those who profess a perfection of Charity ought to aspire. For, as Theology teaches, only perfect is he in whom nothing is lacking, and those who are content with this degree of sanctity lack many things, as we shall see. So in this sense, it is understood—something you may not know—that you may be a saint, but not yet perfect, because more is required for Perfection than for Sanctity.

"The perfect sanctity of which we have been speaking, then—to which we dwellers in this borough ought to aspire—consists in a pure and supremely firm application of our whole soul, acts, and potential toward God, as our Supreme Lord. This includes essentially two things: the first is purity of soul; the second is an immovable union with God, using our entire potential. It follows that the more at one we become with God, the more purity we have, then the more sanctity we shall enjoy.

"Thus, just as with the other virtues, there were always three degrees—the beginners, the proficient, and the perfect—the same three are found in the pursuit of perfect sanctification. First is the immovable Purifying Union with God; second is the immovable Illuminative Union with God; third, the immovable Perficient Union with God. In the first degree, a soul—united with its creator like the purest fountain, purged of the dregs of sin—is first purified. In the second degree, it is united in even greater union, expelling from itself all other affection; it becomes more and more enlightened with new grace and favor. In the third degree, completely pure and united with its creator amidst great floods of love, it becomes more and more perfected.

"Pilgrim, this is perfect Sanctity, and these are the degrees that are ascended by those who truly desire to be Saints. You do your part, for it is not as difficult as it appears, and I, with the grace of the Lord, will help you.

"Now the second thing you wanted to know—what is Contemplation? It is well for you to know how to prepare to receive such an excellent gift from the hand of God. Contemplation is an elevation of soul suspended in God when it becomes as able as it can to enjoy the rapture of eternal sweetness.

"It has four properties. The first one is called Admiration and, by another name, Reverential Fear; the second is Devotion; the third, Suspension; the fourth is Delight, which some call Sweetness. Three degrees are found in those who have written on this matter, and only those who have experienced these states can worthily explain them.

"The first degree is a singular elevation of the soul to God, with a certain congruence of all its powers, caused by the force of divine love. The second is what we call Rest, and by another name, Sleep—not lazy sleep, but operative sleep, which is born from a sweetness that the soul feels in its intimate union with God. The third is called Suspension and normally happens in two ways: first, through ecstasy; second, by rapture. Now ecstasy happens when all our powers—both inner and physical—are absorbed in God and united in a superior and divine bond in a mode beyond the customary way that nature works. Rapture occurs when, by the force of this union, not only the soul, but the body, too, is suspended, carried off by the intensity of the soul.

"The means by which God communicates the gift of contemplation to His friends are, besides through physical aids and illustrations, the seven Gifts of the Holy Spirit: Wisdom, Understanding, Knowledge, Counsel, Fortitude, Piety, and Fear of God. That is why only God can be the cause of our Contemplation. For our part, we can predispose ourselves through the exercise of all the virtues, principally of Prayer and Mortification."

～

CHAPTER X

How Predestined learned perfect sanctity.

These seemed like lofty things to Predestined's humble heart. Driven by an ardent desire to achieve Perfect Sanctity, he humbly asked the Holy Virgin Charity if it was possible for him, a miserable sinner, to reach such excellence.

"For you, Pilgrim, who have arrived at your present state, it is not only possible, it is easy. Because for all those who have managed to find true Disillusionment—like you discovered in Bethlehem, and through the exercise of piety and devotion you learned to live in Nazareth; through the obedience you learned in Bethany; through the divine precepts you found along the way you traveled in Capernaum, or in the Field of Penance; and, finally, as you were able to enter into Bethel, the House of God, spending time in the two boroughs you have lived in here—it is easy to arrive at this last borough of the perfect and in it find Perfect Sanctity."

Predestined rejoiced at her word and begged Charity to perfect that which was begun in him, for the love of that Lord whom he served. This she did and sent Predestined to those two ministers of hers, Prayer and Mortification, whom we have mentioned, to give him final instructions. Furthermore, she sent to him a young maiden of her confidence, named Heart Guard, to be his constant warning of anything that might impede his progress.

The two Holy Sisters first counseled him how he should leave his office and occupation as farmer and return often to the first neighborhood, on Purgative Way, in order to maintain cleanliness, to continually purify his soul, and to watch and examine the fountains to see that they ran pure. For this, he ought to use the counsel and industry of that holy young maiden Heart Guard. If he should find anything contaminated or broken, he would repair it by the precepts that they, Prayer and Mortification, had taught him. Additionally, he should often visit the second neighborhood on Illuminative Avenue, making sure to cultivate and keep fresh the plants he saw there, watering them with the dew from Heaven through the precepts of Prayer, and pruning them according to the instructions of Mortification, protecting them from the foxes in the land and from the birds in the air—for these are contrary works and thoughts, according to the doctrines of Heart Guard.

The two sisters also taught Predestined that his principal preoccupation in this borough was the customary one of industrious farmers. Every day he was to be sure to bring some fruit from the orchard and some flowers from the garden for Charity and for her sons, Love of God and Love of Neighbor, especially the flowers with which she usually adorns herself and the fruits that sustain her. One caution though: let the fruit be picked by the hand of his firstborn children, Good Desire and Upright Intention, because neither Charity nor her children like fruit picked by any other hand.

That is what Pilgrim did, occasionally offering to Charity the flowers he picked, which were the most ardent desires for all the virtues, when, for some reason, he could not practice them. Other times he offered the branches that he pruned; these were the holy intentions with which he undertook all his works, by the supernatural motivation of all the virtues, or glory of God. Yet other times he offered the fruits that are generous and heroic acts of all the virtues, in which Charity herself finds sustenance, and by which her sons, Love of God and Love of Neighbor, find nourishment.

Beyond that, because he worked as a laborer, his sustenance was found in the third branch of that tree Spiritual Life they call Unitive. The two Holy Sisters told him how to make from the leaves and flowers—called Intentions and Effects of Divine Love—a cordial that had the virtue of both refreshing the heart from the flames of profane love and reducing that love to coals in conflagrations of divine love. From the fruits, called Holy Works, they showed him how to distill an oil, called Charity, of such admirable virtue that it cleans the heart of every spot of guilt, and it removes every sign of the scars left by sin; it comforts the heart and gives spiritual strength and beautifies the soul, making it pleasing and friendly to God and, finally, uniting it with its creator.

∽

CHAPTER XI

How Charity took Predestined to her cell, and how she served him,
and what favors she bestowed upon him there.

The Holy Virgin Charity was so satisfied with the devout conformity of Predestined's work — so grateful was she for the flowers and fruit that had become
his daily offering — that she decided to take him to her house, as a sign of that
gratitude, and show him her wine cellar. There she bestowed a thousand favors
upon him and ordained him with Charity, according to the order which Charity herself teaches. There she gave him that cup of wine tempered with the juice
of the pomegranate, which is His Divine Love that was promised him in the
second chapter of the Song of Solomon. Sometimes she gave him milk from her
breast; other times wine from the cup. But he liked the milk better because he
found more sweetness in it. And that is why it is said that her breasts were better than wine.

She took him for walks in the fields, which is the honest recreation that
Charity permits the servants of God to enjoy. Other times she took him to her
orchard, and there she gave him both old and new fruits, which beforehand she
had set aside. It is true that occasionally she would mix green fruit with ripe
fruit, and sweet fruit with bitter fruit, both of which he gladly received. Because
even though the sweet, mature fruit was tastier, the green, bitter fruit was more
profitable.

The one thing that the Holy Virgin was most careful to do was to encourage
a close relationship between Predestined and her sons, Love of God and Love of
Neighbor. At her behest, they spent much time together so that, by and by, they
were hardly ever apart. This friendship grew so strong that one day, when she had
taken him to her garden, that is, when she had done him a thousand favors, she
offered him her breasts as was promised him in the seventh chapter [of the Song
of Solomon], so that he might suckle the milk of her sweetness to his heart's
content, and see how tender was the Lord. And to put a seal upon all those favors, after having celebrated the most chaste of marriage vows — something God
does customarily with the souls of the Just — inviting him to her flowered bed,
supporting his head with her left hand and with her right hand embracing him
(in the same way that the holy soul of Predestined is described in the Song of
Solomon), she caused to come upon him that most gentle sleep of Contemplation, which God reserves for His greatest friends. She warned the daughters of
Zion — or cares of this world — not to wake him or disturb him, so that, with
all his faculties joined in ecstasy with God through the bond of that mysterious
sleep, he might enjoy the sweetness and, in that Contemplation, learn the secrets
that God often communicates to His chosen ones.

But Predestined was a Pilgrim, and he needed to continue on his way toward
Jerusalem, the happy end of his pilgrimage. So Charity, in her great largesse,

filled his gourd with wine — that is, filled his heart with Divine Love — and in his knapsack she placed the beautiful flowers and delicious fruits that delight and feed the inhabitants of Bethel.

~

CHAPTER XII

Some dictates of Divine Love and Perfection that Charity shared with Predestined.

Do not allow an unbridled love of anything in this life, and by and by a great love of God will awaken within you. Do not consider it a small thing to close the doors of your heart to creatures in order to open them to the Creator, because you will be better accompanied by just one Creator than by all creatures together. He who is capable of loving God is capable of more than a little love. Not everyone can achieve great mortification or work great, heroic works for the salvation of others, but all can love God mightily.

The idiot may not know much nor the infirm be capable of much work, but both may love God — and often the humble idiot can love God better than the presumptuous wise man, and the infirm patient better love Him than the robust volunteer.

He who loves much, accomplishes much; but much love is not found in doing much, but in doing what God commands. What does it matter if a slave works the whole year without ceasing, if it is contrary to the will of his Master? Loving and suffering are one eternal round in the philosophy of love, because in the philosophy of divine love, loving is the consequence of suffering, and suffering is the argument for love.

You may not have time to accomplish much work, but you cannot lack time to love much. Because, while your exterior person works physically, you can be doing many acts of love inside: this is the difference there is in our actions, exterior acts are done alone, but acts done with and for the love of God resonate with all.

Like fire is fed with kindling, the love of God endures through good works. What does the spark matter that you get from repeated strikes of the flint if you don't catch it in the wick and then feed it with charcoal? It is the same with the love of God.

Patience is proven through true love. He loves more who suffers more than he who accomplishes many works. God loved the world more redeeming it than creating it; He created the world through works, but He redeemed it through patience.

Hate overcomes when offended; love, through suffering. It is the heart that loves, like David's tower that held only shields and no lances: shields to receive blows, but not lances to offend another.

Richard of Saint Victor said it well: "To be fine, the love of God must be inseparable, insuperable, unsociable, and insatiable: inseparably enduring, insuperable in suffering, unsociable in wanting, and insatiable in working."

Predestined Pilgrim and His Brother Reprobate

PART VI

CHAPTER I

Of Reprobate's last journey.

We find our two Pilgrims on the last journey of their pilgrimage. Although both have traveled that road called Eternity, they did not use the same highways and byways; Predestined always followed the way of Reason, and Reprobate that of Self-Will. Predestined found a shortcut to life, and Reprobate followed the road to eternal death. Reprobate followed his path until he came to a very narrow passage called Transit, or Death. Euphemisms cannot hide the anxiety and affliction that filled him. There he was, in that cramped passage, with such immense burden of riches, servants, and family. Moreover, he was so unaccustomed to work, due to his life of depravity and licentiousness, that he found great difficulties in the passageway and even greater dangers in the passing.

He did pass on, nevertheless—for all do, eventually—and he found himself in the Valley of Josaphat, where there was a tribunal set up by order of God Himself, whom they call the Judge. Reprobate was hoping to rest from his fearful passage when suddenly he was confronted by a severe sheriff, or inspector, of the land called Particular Judge, of whom Reprobate grew noticeably afraid. This Judge came accompanied by three pages named Exam, Charge, and Reward. In their hands were three books, the first of which was the Book of the Past, the second book was the Book of the Present, and the third was the Book of the Future. The first book contained his account, and this was carried by Exam; the second one was carried by Charge, and it detailed his expenses; Reward carried the third book, and in it was a record of the advances and the profit. Besides these books, Particular Judge carried a ledger in which were written all the names of the Predestineds and the Reprobates. By order of the Supreme Judge, no passport would be issued to any pilgrim who came through that was not a Reprobate; for the Kingdom of Babylon was only for Reprobates and not for Predestineds. As soon as Particular Judge laid eyes on Reprobate, he recognized from what the man wore and by the looks of his family that he was a Reprobate. Nevertheless, to make sure, he ordered Exam to give him a good scrutiny, making sure to confirm that the man bore the twelve signs of Reprehension that Reprobates usually carry. The signs were known as the twelve *R*s (an appropriate sign for a Reprobate), which marked certain parts of the body and indicated the state of the soul. The first *R* was found on the forehead; the second, on the back; the third and fourth, on the ears; the fifth, on the hands; the sixth, on the feet; the rest on the heart.

The first *R* on the forehead signified dead faith or faith without works; for it did not mean much to claim faith in Christ and be Predestined's brother, if he did not do the works of a Christian or follow the footsteps of his brother. The *R* on the back represented a hatred of the Cross of Christ, for all his life he had fled tribulations and penance, and had sought only the gastronomy of delight. The *R*s on the ears meant, one, that he had abandoned his first vocation and, two, that he had been an enemy to hearing the word of God. The fifth *R*, on the hands, signified greediness with regard to the poor, for God had given him much wealth, but he had not succored the poor in Christ in their necessities. The sixth *R* on the feet showed how little one had kept the Commandments of God, because any time an occasion of slight temptation arose or one of soliciting human respect, he did not hesitate to compromise divine precepts.

He had six other *R*s impressed on his heart: one showed an anxiousness for wealth, another the spirit of revenge, a third showed the boredom he felt with spiritual things, yet another the apathy he felt for his neighbors, the last one signified the little love and devotion he had for the Most Holy Virgin Mary, Mother of God, and, moreover, that he harbored no affection for any particular Saint.

Once he had seen all twelve signs of Reprehension, Particular Judge determined that the Pilgrim was, in fact, a Reprobate, so he consulted his ledger, that Book of Life wherein the names of all the Predestineds are written. He found that Reprobate's name was not on the list. Therefore, he issued him a sign or passport for Babylon which was similar in style to those words that Saint John wrote in the Apocalypse: *"Non est inventus in libro vitae,"* which means, this Pilgrim's name is not written in the Book of Life. With this document tucked against his heart for safekeeping, he began following a hard trail called Final Sentence, until he found the gates of Babylon.

CHAPTER II

How Reprobate entered Babylon and there was received.

Reprobate ultimately entered Babylon without any problem whatsoever, because its wide gates are open night and day for folks to enter but are always closed for those who wish to leave. He came to a wide field named Gehenna, which means Valley of Sadness. He was presented by the Majordomo Satan to the Governor, or Prince of Babylon, Beelzebub, who checked his passport and delivered guest Reprobate to his Ministers, the Demons, who found him lodging in a very dark neighborhood of the city, where the sun never shines. Christ, in the gospels, called it Outer Darkness—and it is also commonly called Hell—where he could experience the delights that are customary in Babylon.

Since in the Republic of Babylon there is no order whatsoever, but rather eternal horror and confusion, Reprobate nevertheless observed to the letter the Law of God that is in the Apocalypse: the more you enjoy delights during your life, the greater shall be your torment and punishment. And, in strict adherence to that law, Beelzebub's Ministers took hold of the miserable pilgrim as though he were a great millstone, and threw him into a sea of fire, where he was covered with eternal flames as though in an abyss.

So that his torments were proportional to his pleasures, according to the Law of Babylon, for Reprobate had spent his whole life luxuriating in the pleasures of the flesh and in sensual delights, at that same moment horrendous demonic visions began to torment his sight: blasphemies against the Creator assaulted his ears; the intolerable smells of the place filled his nostrils; the gall and bitterness of Hell saturated his taste; the teeth of infernal serpents stung his sense of touch. Sometimes he was fried in oil. Other times he was bathed in molten ore. On occasion they pierced his heart a thousand times, yet he did not die. Or the dragons pulled him into a thousand pieces. In sum, Reprobate suffered every conceivable torment and punishment, without remedy, without relief, and without surcease.

To entertain Reprobate in this terrible prison, Punishment of the Damned used to send his page, Eternal Opprobrium, who repeated continually to him those words of David: "*Ecce homo, qui non possuit Deum adjutorem praevaluit in vanitate sua*," which means: behold that man Reprobate, Predestined's brother, who placed all his trust in the vanity of the world, and not in God, his Creator. Behold how late he discovered the illusion of the Way of Vanity. On the heels of this little devil Punishment sent him a serpent of terrible countenance called Beast of Your Own Conscience, who encircled him with a thousand coils called Imaginings, and with three teeth it pierced his heart. The three teeth were named Memory, Understanding, and Will, and they did torment him much. Will pierced his heart with eternal obstinacy and desperation and caused him to utter a thousand blasphemies against the Creator. Memory bit into his heart with a cognizance of the brevity and foulness of the delights for which he had lost the Kingdom of Heaven and earned those torments. Understanding cut into his heart with a representation of his Brother Predestined, who was joyfully awaiting entry at the Gates of Jerusalem.

"Oh, my Brother Predestined," he would say, "how happy your luck has been, and how cursed is mine! How right you were to travel toward Jerusalem by way of life's Disillusionment, and how wrong I was to follow the Road of Vanity to Babylon! Oh, cursed be Self-Will, who deceived me, and accursed be my children, who relieved me of my senses to journey through Beth-Aven, and not, like you, through Bethlehem! How easily I could have been as blessed as you have been, if I, like you, had followed the path of Reason! But in my affliction, I feel my mistake; I already see the fruit of my imprudence; I already suffer eternally the punishment for my sins."

With these and other words full of wrath and confusion did he voice the eternal wailing and gnashing of teeth that Christ foretells in the gospels; that miserable, condemned Reprobate suffers to this day, and so shall he continue to do for as long as God is God, for all eternity.

These desperate words found their way to the ears of his Brother Predestined, and with a greatly disturbed heart, they say he spoke these words: "Behold, oh, poorly counseled Brother, the place where the wrongful steps of your pilgrimage have led you. For this is the end of your journey, the conclusion of your sordid life, the prize for your imprudence, the fruit of your labors or the punishment for your sins. Behold how, from among the delights and pastimes of a brief life, you have cultivated eternal torments of Hell. The vanities are gone that you followed in Beth-Aven; so are the vices and profanities of Samaria. The libertine life you professed in Betheron is over. Edom's voluptuousness and delights have ended. Babel's confusion has been confirmed. Look hard on this: all of your pastimes have become eternal torments, and all your hopes, eternal confusion.

"Behold, most imprudent one, how for a bowl of pottage you have sold your birthright to Heaven, and how for a brief delight you have lost eternal happiness. See how you lost everything, hoping to hold on to so very little. There go the honors; there go the riches; there go the delights. Those occasions to sin that you so anxiously sought for are no more. Your delights have arranged these torments; your unchastity has cast you into this lake of fire; the pride in your life has directed you to this eternal confusion. Desperately you bewail so much misery, yet you will not leave this place for all eternity. Heaven's Gate is now forever closed to you. You no longer need to hope for the Mercy of God nor for the blood of Jesus Christ that He shed for you. For now that Holy Cosmographer, the Angel of God, has abandoned you forever. Now that most Pure Virgin, who is there for all sinners, can no longer help you. This is what you wanted; here you must suffer endlessly throughout eternity. A thousand years from now, this is where you will be. In a hundred thousand years, you will still be here. A hundred thousand million years from now, this is where you will be. For all eternity, you will suffer here, without relief, without redress."

∼

CHAPTER III

Of the Holy City of Jerusalem, the happy end of Predestined's journey.

This was the lamentable end of the Pilgrim Reprobate. And this shall be the end of all those who follow in his footsteps. Another, very different end befell his brother Predestined. One of the great blessings that the Lord gave him in that vine-clad chamber in Bethel, as we mentioned, was to reveal to Predestined how close he was to the end of his pilgrimage and that from there to the gates of Jerusalem was but a short distance. With that news, Pilgrim waxed exceedingly joyful, for all those days he spent in Bethel in communion with Charity and with Love of God, he also spent nostalgic for Zion, yearning for Jerusalem. Since Love of God had told him of its wonders, of its marvelous citizens, and so many things about the goodness, wisdom, and magnificence of its King, the good Pilgrim cried out those same words as Saint Paul: *"Quis me liberabit de corpore mortis hujus?"*[70] and sighing: *"Cupio dissolvi, et esse cum Christo."*[71]

God finally granted his desires, and, he knew not how, presently he found himself at the gates of Jerusalem. It was of such exotic architecture that only the most eloquent of its citizens could worthily describe it. One of them by the name of John, in his Apocalypse, says that its foundations were twelve of the richest, most precious stones imaginable. Its twelve gates were made of twelve extremely beautiful pearls. The whole City was of fine gold, as resplendent and diaphanous as glass, and all its streets were paved with fine gold, and more transparent than crystal. In it, there was no night or any darkness, because it was always one eternal day or perpetual light. Nor was sunlight necessary to cause the light there because the sun in that blessed city is God himself, and his lamp is the Lamb of God, who is Christ.

Besides the beauty, richness, and excellence of its buildings, the land over which they spread is so large, that the Prophet Baruch calls it immense, magnificent, and endless—capable of housing, besides its own angels, all the Predestined Pilgrims from every place on earth who will meet there. These are so many that they exceed the number of the stars in Heaven and the sands of the sea. Down the middle of it runs a river where all drink, which David called the River of Delights, whose currents, as David himself testifies, immensely gladden this City of God. The climate is so mild and temperate that one feels neither the harshness of winter nor the rigors of summer. Rather it is an eternal spring, exempt from the injuries of time or inclement winds. Its fountains are soothing; honey runs in its rivers. Milk flows in its mountains, and its hills give butter. For Jerusalem is the true Promised Land, the land of milk and honey, by which the Lord meant to suggest the fertility of its land and the mildness of its climate. Put that together with the beauty of its gardens, its exquisite orchards, its exotic flowers; the freshness of its woods; the richness of its valleys; the fragrance of its aromas; the music of its birds mixed together with the burbling of its brooks in such harmony, sweetness, and delight for the senses; for good reason they call it the Paradise of Delights.

The number, order, and nobility of its citizens, the light of its Republic, the peace, the harmony among its dwellers—who can adequately describe it? The principal nobility of the City are its natural citizens, the Angels, who are divided into three orders they call hierarchies. Each order has nine families, or Choirs—all of admirable power, knowledge, and beauty—more numerous than the Stars of Heaven and than the leaves of trees. Just once Ezekiel caught a glimpse and saw ten hundred thousand waiting on the King. For they are all ministers or vassals of his royal palace. From these are drawn the armies of the heavenly hosts with which this city is protected—all soldiers of such valor that

---

[70] "Who shall deliver me from the body of this death?"
[71] "I wish to be dissolved and to be with Christ."

just one of them killed one hundred and eighty-five thousand Assyrians in the camps of Sennacherib.

There are innumerable Citizens who descend from any number of peoples, tribes, and nations, but who all now call Jerusalem their home. The King, out of respect for their works and services rendered to Him, has made them Fellow Citizens in this great City, remembering the nobility of their titles and coats of arms that they used in their respective lands—Prophets, Apostles, Doctors, Martyrs, Confessors, Virgins—and allowing them to use their genealogical crests, by which all know and respect them.

What can I say of the life and daily activity of these sovereign citizens? All live a blessed life, a pure life, a chaste life, a holy life, a glorious life, a life wherein there is no death, no corruption, no sadness, no melancholy, no bother or molestation. It is a life without the changes and vicissitudes of this one: no enemies that inflict fear or compound ailments. All live in the same spirit and love of their King, who is God himself. All live in the same love and spirit of immortal life and blessedness, and this is why this city is called Vision of Peace and City of God.

Now, here was Predestined, at the gates of this sovereign city, desiring mightily to enter it. And, as his heart thumped in his chest, eyes filled with tears, he cried out these words, "God save you, sweet homeland, City of Refuge, Sure Port, Paradise of Delights, Land of the Living, Celestial Palace, Blessed House, Garden of Flowers, Court of Immense Grandeur, Marketplace of All Good Things, and the happy end of my pilgrimage! God save you, Celestial Jerusalem, dwelling place of all Pilgrims, Refuge of the homeless, Victory of the militant, and Crown of the Predestined! By the rivers of Babylon, I sat down one day. And their currents swelled with the tears from my eyes; I sighed for you, oh, Jerusalem, when, oh, Zion, I remembered you! Now, happy, I come to you, for I rejoiced when they said I would go the House of the Lord.

"And you, oh, thrice and a thousand times blessed dwellers of Jerusalem, have you left your exile for your homeland, and your Pilgrim's habit for the stole of glory? I, too, am Predestined just like you; you were Pilgrims just like me. Let me now enter the Homeland of the Predestined, just like you when you lived in the land of the Pilgrims."

～

CHAPTER IV

Of what Predestined accomplished at the Gates of Jerusalem.

Joyfully Predestined was waiting for his hour to enter the gates of such a noble city, to enjoy the fruit of his pilgrimage, when they showed him a corridor — and what a close, fearful one it was! — through which he had to pass: it was that very narrow bridge called Hour of Death, and sometimes Transition. Beneath it ran that valley in Babylon called Gehenna Ignis, inhabited by all the Reprobate Pilgrims. From either side of it blow stiff winds called Temptations, Fears, and Anguish, which Predestined's brother Reprobate had already felt during his crossing.

What made the crossing of this bridge all the more fearful was seeing that almost all the Pilgrims, or the majority of them who planned to cross it, fell off of it, down into the valley in Babylon — Gehenna Ignis — that spread out below. One time, thirty thousand Pilgrims came to cross the bridge. Out of all of them, only five made it across: they were Bernard, Abbot of Clairvaux; a deacon from Lyons; and three other Pilgrims. Another time he saw sixty thousand Pilgrims approach the bridge, and, of that group, only three made it to the other side, while the rest ended up together in that Valley of Hell. Then, with a voice like a trumpet, Predestined exclaimed, "*Cum metu, e tremore salutem vestram operamini!*"[72] and, addressing God from the intimacy of his heart, he said, "*Domine, quis salvus fiat?*"[73]

To which the Lord answered, "*Qui perseveraverit usque in finem, hic salvus erit.*"[74]

"And who is brave enough," answered Predestined, "to make it across such a terrible bridge with so much danger of falling?"

"Whosoever is a Pilgrim in the world and dresses in the manner of a Pilgrim — like you," answered the Lord. "Do you not see how all these pilgrims you have seen fall into the Valley of Hell — although they call themselves Pilgrims — are *not* Pilgrims, either in their dress or in their style of life? Have you not seen what bizarre clothing some wear, how others come loaded with treasures, how others are followed by multitudes of servants, and others are weighed down with a thousand trunks? Have you seen how some who look like Pilgrims did not really live like Pilgrims, for they have forgotten their true homeland, Jerusalem, thinking only of Egypt, which is the world? How is it possible, with such pomp and impediment, to cross safely to the other side of the bridge without such conspicuous danger of falling?"

---

[72] "With fear and trembling, work out your salvation."

[73] "Lord, who can be saved?"

[74] "He who constantly perseveres to the end of the bridge, he is the one who shall be saved."

Predestined's spirit soared as he listened to the Lord's words; he remembered how all his life he had been a Pilgrim, having never considered this life other than an exile, and how, presently, through the mercies of the Lord, he was still in Pilgrim's clothing, living the same Pilgrim's life that he had been living when he left Egypt. Deep in his heart grew a great confidence of crossing safely to the other side of the bridge. Except for his Pilgrim's clothing, Predestined would take only his knapsack of good works, for he knew very well that anything else was useless on the other side of the bridge. So, in an orderly fashion, he wished to arrange things in such a way that his memory would not be troubled in the crossing. He counseled with his wife, Reason, and prepared a sealed document, commonly called a Testament. In it he arranged his affairs with such clarity and exactness that his conscience became imperturbably calm.

Free of that preoccupation, he carefully examined the journey of his pilgrimage, sorting through his Pilgrim's gear. First he checked his backpack, gourd, and staff—the principal signs of the pilgrim: the Staff called Fortitude; the wine gourd of Spiritual Comfort, which is Prayer; the knapsack of Good Works. With that preparation, although he felt the fear that all Pilgrims experience in this passing, and with the names of Jesus and Mary on his lips and in his heart, he passed safely to the other side of the bridge.

≈

CHAPTER V

Of Predestined's rigorous exam they gave Predestined before he entered Jerusalem.

As soon as he arrived at the other side of the bridge, he was met by that severe Inspector called Particular Judge, accompanied by all his pages: Exam, Charge, and Reward, who carried their customary Books of Receipt, Expense, and Profit, that are used on such occasions. As soon as he recognized Pilgrim, he detained him and with booming voice asked what he wished.

"To enter this Holy City," he answered, "To be one of its dwellers."

"Do you not know what Saint John says? That into this Holy City goes no one with even a spot of sin? Do you not know that its dwellers can be no one but the Predestined alone?"

In his fear, Pilgrim was able to say that by the goodness of the Lord he was Predestined, although about spot of sin he did not know, though he feared that as a sinner he might have many. So Particular Judge called for a Scrutinous Exam to see if Pilgrim carried the twelve signs of the Predestined—those twelve crosses on various parts of the body, marked according to the significance of each one.

The first cross was impressed upon his forehead, the second on the back, the third on the ears, two on the hands, two on the feet, and five on the heart. The forehead cross was the sign of a living Faith, or faith with works. The second cross meant the love of Christ's cross and that a person had patiently suffered tribulations in this life. The third one on the ears showed a person to have been a friend of listening to the word of God. Of the two on the hands, one meant that a person had shown compassion to the poor, and the other signified a heroic effort to leave the world and follow the way of gospel perfection. The two crosses on the feet symbolized the keeping of the divine precepts and partaking of the sacraments. Of the five crosses impressed upon the heart, the first was charity toward God and neighbors, the second was resignation to the will of God, the third was humbleness of heart, the fourth confirmed one's meekness of spirit, the fifth indicated a cordial love and devotion to the sovereign Virgin, Mother of God. All these signs are those of the Predestined in this life, and by them can be conjectured who is Predestined for eternal life. Exam found all or most of them on Pilgrim. Therefore, Particular Judge pronounced him morally Predestined. But, because these signs were not infallible—for on a number of occasions he had even discovered them on many Reprobates—in order to be very sure, he opened the Book of Life that he carried with him. He read the words of Saint John from the Apocalypse: *"Qui scripti sunt in libro vitae."*[75] With that consultation the happy Pilgrim was recognized as Predestined.

Once this was accomplished, Judge moved to another very important examination to see if Predestined had paid his tribute they call the mortal one, with the coin called Final Grace and Satisfaction of Sin. One cannot enter without paying this tribute. For no citizen, no matter how noble, is exempt from that payment, which coin is equal in value to that money which the Lord in the gospel called Denarius of Glory. When placed on a scale, it weighs as much as the weight of eternal glory, as Saint Paul writes. For when the Lord minted the seals or crosses of his Passion, he stamped upon them the worth of His merits and the infinite price of His blood.

After this, Particular Judge opened the Book of Life Past which Exam handed him, and he read off all the sins Predestined had committed throughout his whole life, as well as the blessings received from God. On the sin side, he had on many occasions broken the Commandments of God and His church and had lost his baptismal grace. On the blessings side, he saw how God had raised him, kept him, called him to grace, and redeemed him with His Blood, providing for him many, many useful ways to be saved, especially through the Seven Sacraments.

In the second Book of Life Present, brought by Charge, he saw what he had done to acquit himself: how he had left Egypt and its vanity; how he had become disillusioned with the world in Bethlehem; how he had lived piously and religiously in Nazareth; how he had observed the Law of God in Bethany; how he had done penance in Capernaum; how he had sought perfection in Bethel.

---

[75] "Who/of which are written in the Book of Life."

In the third Book of Life Future, carried by Reward, he saw that all his works were worthy of eternal reward, and he, by them, was worthy to enter Jerusalem and become one of its citizens.

He saw that for every meritorious work, there is a corresponding prize which only in that Holy City is awarded with justice and faithfulness.

Judge found, however, that since Predestined had strayed upon occasion from Bethel's path, or the way to perfection, that he had fallen a number of times, although with no serious injury, along the Way of the Commandments, and that even now he bore some spots. And since it is not possible to enter Jerusalem with spots, Particular Judge sent Predestined to a Bath called Purgatory in order to become completely clean and purified.

∽

CHAPTER VI

Of the terrible bath taken in Purgatory by Predestined.

Near the fields of Gehenna, or Valley of Sadness, is a certain valley or immense concavity called Purgatory. According to some authors, it is in the district or province of Babylon. Through it runs a sea of fire so terrible and active that elementary fire, by comparison, is but a painting of its intensity. The care of this molten bath is entrusted to two severe but very holy maidens; both are daughters of Divine Justice. One is called Punishment of Condemnation; the other is Punishment of Sense. No Pilgrim named Reprobate can enter therein, because as terrible as that place is, it was designated by the most merciful King of Jerusalem exclusively for Predestined Pilgrims, in order to purify them, like gold in a crucible.

Our Predestined stepped into it, and, as though he were seeing a freshly drawn bath of water, he dove into that immense pool of glowing fire, because he was sure it was the will of God, and that from this bath he would emerge to an eternal refreshment and to the delights that awaited him in Jerusalem. Once he was in, the two Sisters began to perform their office. Such was the bath given him by Punishment of Sense that all the pains of the Holy Martyrs and even those suffered by Christ pale by comparison. Only then did Predestined realize by his own experience that which he had read in Gershon: that one hour in Purgatory was more rigorous than one hundred years of penance in this life.

Although the bath that Punishment of Sense gave Predestined was indeed atrocious, worse yet was the one given him by Punishment of Condemnation. Because one moment's absence from the clear sight of the Creator, for which he anxiously yearned, was for him greater than all the torments of Hell. He had been in this place not more than an hour, yet it seemed to him that many years had passed. Amidst these torments, Pilgrim also received much consolation from three Holy Maidens: Faith, Hope, and Charity, who visited him frequently and consoled him with sweet, soothing words. Charity assured him that he could not now fall from the Grace and Love of God because he had already been confirmed in grace, united eternally by love with his Creator. Hope certified that his entrance into Jerusalem was certain and that it was now impossible not to be one of its citizens. Faith revealed to him just how much the King desired to see him and enjoy with him in His Palace those intercessions to which all the Citizens had continuous claim, particularly through the Queen Mother, who ceaselessly prayed for him and all the other Pilgrims suffering in that same bath.

Predestined also found much consolation in the company of the other Pilgrims united there in the same spirit, in harmony with the will of the Lord, recognizing the great mercies that He had bestowed on them. Although, for the errors of his pilgrimage, he thought he might deserve the eternal confusion of Babylon, he had been blessed with this temporary Purgatory bath. Nevertheless, he saw that almost all of them—like a slave girl who keeps her eyes upon the hands of her mistress—kept their eyes upon our hands, waiting for our intercessory prayers, and repeating now the words of Holy Job: *"Miseremini mei, miseremini mei, saltem vos amici mei,"*[76] now the words of the Prophet Jeremiah: *"O vos omnes, qui transitis per viam: attendite et videte, si est dolor sicut dolor meus."*[77] Predestined saw something remarkable, worthy of mention here. He had approached one of the handsome young Pilgrims whom he judged to be his Guardian Angel. The man told him one of his daughters at that very moment had borne him a grandson in Egypt who would one day be a Priest of God and would offer a sacrifice in his behalf. So he would soon be leaving that Purgatorial bath for the delights of Jerusalem. Pilgrim rejoiced at that news.

He also saw how every year on the fifteenth of August, at the celebration of the glorious Assumption of the Virgin Mary, Mother of God, a woman of admirable majesty and beauty, during the first hour after midnight, would enter that bath and then leave, taking with her a great many of those pilgrims into Jerusalem, where she dwelt. He realized that she was the very Virgin Mother of God, who, in the hour of her ascent into Heaven, was descending into Purgatory to rescue the souls of her devotees and take them with her to the Blessedness of Glory.

Predestined most marveled at many pilgrims there, who in order to wash away even the tiniest spot and purify the most insignificant blemish, stayed in that bath longer than he imagined necessary. He realized how right two holy dwellers in Jerusalem, Jerome and Augustine, had been when they told him

---

[76] "Have pity on me, have pity on me, at least you, my friends."

[77] "O all ye that pass by the way, attend, and see if there be any sorrow like to my sorrow."

that it was a rare thing, indeed, for one to enter Jerusalem without first passing through a bath of fire.

∾

CHAPTER VII

The entrance of Predestined Pilgrim into Jerusalem and how he was received.

Predestined spent just one hour in that terrible bath of Purgatory, and he left it purer than gold from a crucible. Since he had spent so many years in Capernaum — land of penance — and lived so many days in the Valley of Anguish, he had occasion in those places to purify the majority of his blemishes, which lingered from his serious sins in Egypt. Now that the happy hour of his rest was arrived, he passed, without any impediment, through the gates of that Blessed City, which, once the King of Glory had passed through them, were never again shut to any Predestined Pilgrim. But who can explain with words the festive joy, the jubilation, the triumph with which the Pilgrim was received by those Blessed Citizens? Not even Predestined himself, who experienced it, could do it justice if he came from Heaven to earth and preached it to us.

The first to greet him were the dwellers of Jerusalem, both the natives of the land, who are the Angels, and the rest of the Pilgrims, who are the Saints and Courtiers of Glory. The natives came forward divided into three orders, and each order into three choirs. In the first order came the Seraphim, the Cherubim, and the Throne. In the second order came those called Principalities, Dominions, and Powers. In the third order came the ones called Virtues, Archangels, and Angels. Nine choirs strong, these three orders sang the song with which all Pilgrims are received into Jerusalem: *"Euge serve bone et fidelis, quia super pauca fuisti fidelis, supra multa te constituam, intra in gaudium Domini tui."*[78] The Pilgrims who were already Citizens of that Sovereign City, also divided into seven choirs, congratulated his entrance in a thousand ways. The Patriarchs blessed him a thousand times for the success of his pilgrimage. The Prophets announced his entry a thousand times, seeing in him the fulfillment of the promises of their prophecies. The Apostles praised him a thousand times, for they saw him representing the fruit of their preaching. The Doctors, a thousand praises, for he represented the execution of the dictates of their doctrine. The Martyrs sang a thousand triumphs for the happy victory of their battles and for the constant imitation of their tribulations. The Confessors offered him a thousand favors, for he had followed their steps throughout his life, and now he was enjoying their same hap-

---

[78] "Well done, good and faithful servant: because thou hast been faithful over a few things, I will place thee over many things. Enter thou into the joy of thy Lord."

piness. The Virgin Maidens were most joyful to see him follow the path of the Lamb because during his pilgrimage he had tried to follow the example of their purity. All of them, each in his own benevolent way, sang his glory and celebrated his triumph.

The honors, the festivities, the joyful way that the King Himself received Pilgrim—who can tell in words? "Come," He said, "blessed one of My Father, and possess the kingdom which through all eternity has been prepared for you."

With those words, He bid them undress the new Citizen from his Pilgrim's raiment— which are the penalties of this life—and dress him in the stole of glory that David had promised. He dried the tears that Predestined had cried in the Vale of Tears, proclaiming that the hour of crying and lamentation was over because the rigorous Winter of Time had passed, and the flowery Spring of Eternity had already begun.

Upon the stole of glory, He placed the purple of Kings, and with His own hand set upon his head the crown of precious stones that David called honor and glory. In this manner, He made room for him in His own Throne, according to the promise that He had made to the victor.

He bade him sit at His table as a vigilant Servant. Not only was he served by angels, but by the very Lord of all, according to the promise that He had made in the gospel of Saint Luke. "To him that overcometh," He says in the Apocalypse, "will I give to eat of the hidden manna." He drank from that river of delights which gladdens the City of God, and he heard the gentle melody that nine choirs of musicians in the Royal Chapel sang, accompanied by well-tuned instruments. The verse begins: *"Veni de Libano, et coronaberis."*[79]

The Citizen of Jerusalem finds the greatest glory and happiness in the clear countenance of their King and in the enjoyment of his powers and infinite wisdom. Just so the Majesty of the King did for Predestined in the Celestial Jerusalem the same thing that King Hezekiah did for the ambassadors of Berodach in the terrestrial Jerusalem. He celebrated his arrival with much joy, showed him the greatness and majesty of his Palace—principally those three spacious rooms called Immensity, Eternity, and Infinity of God. Like Hezekiah, He showed him His infinite treasures and the immense wealth of His wisdom; He introduced him to the exquisite Library of the lofty secrets of Divine Providence and hidden judgments of God. He showed him that enigma—so dark on earth, so clear in Heaven—of the inscrutable Mystery of the Holy Trinity. He pointed out the works, all marvelous, of Divine Omnipotence; the admirable organization of His Divine Justice; and the infinite treasury of His Mercies. He showed the lustrous appointments of His House and Royal Palace—the Sun, the Moon, the Stars that so beautifully shine upon the outside walls of Royal Palace of Heaven—the bright and noble orders of His Vassals, which compose the three

---

[79] "Come from Libanus, thou shalt be crowned."

Celestial Hierarchies and the nine Choirs of Angels, of which the seven most important stand in constant service of His Majesty the King.

The most marvelous thing is that He did what Hezekiah did not do, and what colleagues usually do for their most intimate friends—He reached deep into his most hidden chamber and shared with him the intimacy of His heart, in which He expressed His love. He showed Pilgrim His dear spouse, that is His most Holy Humanity, in all its radiance and splendor. He showed him his Queen Mother in all her glory and majesty. He revealed the innumerable number of all the children of God who are the Saints and Blessed Partakers of Glory. And finally, all that God has in the treasuries of His palace was made manifest to the Pilgrim; there was nothing that was kept from him. The result was an advantage much greater than Hezekiah had given the ambassadors of Berodach, for not only had He displayed all of His riches, power, and wisdom, but shared them most liberally with the Pilgrim.

First He gave him that gold coin, immensely heavy and of infinite value, that the Lord himself called the Denarius of Glory. He gave him a crown made from a single precious stone, richer and more resplendent than all the jewels of the Orient. He was given that carbuncle stone, or diamond, of inestimable price, called the Light of Glory, of such admirable virtue and splendor that it comforts and illustrates the understanding to be able to know the divinity of God Himself and the secrets of His Holy Wisdom. Predestined was given a jewel to adorn his body, made of four of the finest stones called Glorious Gifts, that is, Imperviousness, Agility, Subtlety, and Clarity—with which he became so handsome and comely that the united beauty of the whole earth could not compare. The first stone has the virtue of sealing Predestined's body so that no contrary quality can bother him, not even the very fire of Hell. The second makes him so agile and swift that he can equal the speed of the swiftest thought. The third one spiritualizes him so that he is able to penetrate the most impenetrable rock without any repugnance or resistance whatsoever—as though he were a spirit and not a body. Finally, the fourth stone makes him so resplendently handsome that he exceeds by seven times the beauty and brilliance of the sun.

This Sovereign King removed all restraint from his honors, favors, and liberality, ordering Predestined Pilgrim to be recorded not only as a Citizen of Jerusalem in Perpetuity, but as His own adopted son, like the others—placing upon him His Holy Name and that of His Eternal Father, according to the truth of His promise, delivering to him the whole inheritance of His kingdom, as an heir of Christ—to live and rule eternally with Him, without any fear or danger of losing Him ever again.

～

CHAPTER VIII

Of what Predestined did and said after some time in Jerusalem.

Confused to the point of distraction, Predestined knew not what to say or feel—seeing himself surrounded by so much joy, esteemed with so many honors, regaled with so many delights—because, although from the Prophets and Doctors, he had heard glorious things about that City of God, he had never conceived its greatness to be that which he now personally experienced. He saw that he was surrounded on every side by a Sea of Delights; he saw himself honored by all the courtiers and dwellers of Glory; he saw himself enriched by the treasures of Heaven; he saw himself pass from abject misery to the highest form of happiness—from Pilgrim to Citizen, from servant to lord, from slave to King—with an Endowment from the King of Heaven. And he saw that all the Citizens of that Holy City wore crowns, held scepters, and were dressed in purple.

His heart was pounding with joy, and if in that glorious place there was any room for confusion, it was possible that one might be confused by how so few services could earn one so many rewards. Prostrate before the Sovereign Majesty of that King, he kissed His hand a thousand times, expressing a thousand thanks from the intimacy of his heart.

"Oh, King of Glory!" he said. "Oh, Sovereign Prince! What have you seen in me for so much honor? What have I done to deserve such reward? What tribulations have I endured that I enjoy such rest? What penances did I do to be recompensed with so many delights? You, you, oh, Sovereign King, you with your cross made me worthy of this Blessedness. You with your pain and suffering acquired these delights. With your humility you obtained this Glory—with your opprobrium, these honors; with your death, this life. Infinite are the thanks I give you for such mercy. Angels praise you; let all the Saints of your House praise you, and may this, your servant, praise you, too. For through your infinite goodness, you have raised him to the status of Son of God.

"And you, oh, pure Virgin, oh, Mother of My Lord! By your intercession, I have come to this place, and by your protection I have received this great boon. What would have become of me had it not been for you? You sustained me on my pilgrimage as my Lady; you were my powerful defender; you made intercession for me as my advocate; you guided my way like a star; you loved me like a mother; you obtained for me so much good as the universal benefactress of all humanity.

"And you, oh, Sovereign Spirit, oh, Guardian Angel, what thanks do I owe you for directing me toward so much good? You freed me from danger; you led me away from temptations; you watched over all the paths of my salvation; through all the discourse of my pilgrimage you were my Guide, Angel, Teacher, Lord, and Companion, and though I was many times ungrateful for your angelic presence, you never abandoned me until restoring me to this Blessed Homeland and place of happiness.

"And you, oh, Blessed Citizens of the City of God, by your intercessions I have become your companion in your glory. Your examples inspired me to follow your steps; the remembrance of your felicity caused me to seek your company; the happy end of your pilgrimage made me pursue my own until its end; like you, I fought the battles of the Lord; now, like you, I enjoy the triumph of victory; I was, like you, a Pilgrim, but like you, I am now a Citizen."

CHAPTER IX

Predestined's exhortation to the Pilgrims of this life.

Predestined was absorbed in the possession of his joy. However, the charity of such saintly citizens does not permit the forgetting of the Pilgrims still in exile who travel astray from the true path to Jerusalem—or who are at least at risk of making wrong turns and becoming lost. With a voice of thunder that all could understand, he said, "Oh, Pilgrims, you who in the exile of this life live so forgetful of your sweet homeland—oh, you who live in the little valleys of Babylon, so forgetful of Zion—open your eyes and behold the happy end of my pilgrimage. Take heart to follow in my path so you might be a companion to my fortune. Remember that you are Pilgrims and you have no permanent city there, because your homeland is this one that I now enjoy—not the one in which you live. Do not take your exile to be your homeland, nor your pilgrimage to be your rest. If you could know how sweet a Patria awaits you, how magnificent its palaces are, how innumerable its mansions, how organized its Republic, how peaceful its dwellers, how kind and gentle its Lord.

"If you could hear the hidden words that I have heard—which eye cannot see and ear cannot hear, nor can the heart of man receive—that God has prepared for those who love Him! Oh, if you could know the immense sea of joy that the Lord has reserved for his faithful servants! True is what Anselm told you anciently: *"Gaudium erit intra, gaudium erit extra, gaudium sursum, et gaudium deorsum."*[80] Oh, if you could taste just one drop of water from the River of Delights of this sweet homeland, how bitter Egypt's turbid waters would seem to you! If you could taste the honey and butter of this Promised Land, how plain would Egypt's garlic and onions become!

"How brief, how dirty, how false are all the delights, honors, and riches of that life! How solid, how pure, how true are those of this life! *Mendaces filii hominum in stateris.*[81] They wish to weigh in the balance eternal things, which

---

[80] "Joy will be within, joy will be outside, and joy all around."

[81] "On balance, all the Pilgrims of that life are deceivers, for they know not how to properly weigh things as they ought."

they cannot grasp, against the temporal ones that they enjoy—and they never do discover the worth of first. They ought, rather, to weigh temporal things against eternal ones; for if they do, they will soon discover how insane, how light and worthless they all are. So, Pilgrims, what are you careless people doing in your exile? Have you not heard what Cypriano is telling you: "*Patriam nostram Paradisum computemus, parentes Patriarchas jam habere caepimus, quid non properamos, & currimus, ut patriam nostram videre, & parentes salutare possimus?*"[82]

Perhaps the difficulty of the road has detained you, or the impossibility of entry? You do not have to fear the road after Christ has shown the way and after so many Pilgrims followed that path. Do you not see so many tender young maidens, so many dear children, and so many tired elders following after Christ with their crosses, which are their Pilgrims' staffs—how all arrive, and all enter? "*Curramos, et sequamur Christum,*" Saint Gregory tells us—Run and follow Christ! Saint Jerome warns us: "*Nullus labor durus, quo gloria aeternitatis acquiritur.*"[83]

But I want to warn you, oh, Pilgrims, that what Saint Bernard said was not hyperbole when he preached during his sojourn with you in your exile that if it were necessary to suffer great torments daily—and suffer just briefly the torments of Hell—just to see the King of this Celestial Jerusalem and to be one of its Citizens, that would be an insignificant work for so great a glory. Oh, Pilgrims, do not think this to be hyperbole, for by my own experience, I know what Saint Paul testifies to be true: "*Non sunt condignae passiones hujus saeculi ad futuram gloriam, quae revelabitur in nobis.*"[84]

~

CHAPTER X

Conclusion of the complete history of Predestined Pilgrim and his brother Reprobate.

Behold, devout Reader, the end had by our Predestined Pilgrim to all his travels; herein you have seen the destination of his pilgrimage. Now it will be good for you to compare his consequence with the fate of his Brother Reprobate, so that by looking at the success of the one and the other you might examine the life you lead, in order to know the end that awaits you. For in this life we are all Pilgrims, and one day there shall be an end to our pilgrimage. That end will be either eter-

---

[82] "Our homeland is Paradise, our parents are Patriarchs. Why not go look for your homeland and greet your parents?"

[83] "The path is not difficult if it is the one that leads to eternal glory."

[84] "No hardships in your pilgrimage will ever be greater than the rest and refreshment in the Homeland that awaits you."

nal salvation or eternal condemnation. If you wish to know which of these two destinies awaits you, examine the way you make your journey. If you are following Predestined's steps, you can expect salvation in the end; if you are following in the steps of Reprobate, you can surely fear a destiny of condemnation.

You have seen well, oh, pious Reader, how Reprobate left Egypt with good intentions in the company of his Brother Predestined—how, deceived by Self-Will, he abandoned the company of his good Brother and traveled through Beth-Aven, House of Vanity. He then went to the lands of Ephraim to live in Samaria, Land of Idolaters and Sinners. From there he traveled through the cursed mountains of Gelboe, which means Puffed-Up in Pride, and went to live in Bethoron, or House of License. From Bethoron he made his way through those delicious lands this side of Jordan, and found lodging in the land of Edom, which means voluptuousness. After that he went through the fields of Sanaar and arrived in Babel, or confusion—land of sins, where badness rules. Finally from there straight to Babylon, figure of Hell, where he was given citizenship in perpetuity, and became a subaltern of Beelzebub, Prince of Demons and Governor of Hell.

On the other hand, oh, Reader, you have seen how his Brother Predestined followed Reason's counsel and traveled through Bethlehem, House of Bread—now City of Disillusionment after the Truth of God was born there. How from Bethlehem he followed the path of Christ and dwelt in Nazareth, Land of Religion. And from there to Bethany, House of Obedience, where, by Way of the Commandments, he came to rest in Capernaum, Field of Penance. After spending a long time in the Valley of Tribulations, he came to the Holy City of Bethel, House of God and City of Perfection, where Charity governs. And from there he came to Jerusalem, the happy destination of his pilgrimage, where he lives eternally with his King, who is Christ our Savior, as one of his Blessed Citizens.

Now I ask you this—you who read that which I represent here in parable —is this not what truly happens to us? Is it not true that we are all brothers, children of the same Father, who is God? Is it not true that all of us in this life, for as long as we shall live in it, are like Pilgrims, or exiles? Is not our Homeland Heaven and the earth but an exile? Is it not a faithful thing that of all of us who are Pilgrims, some are Reprobates and some are Predestined? Were not Cain and Abel both brothers and both Pilgrims—one Reprobate and one Predestined? Were not Jacob and Esau both brothers, sons of the same father and the same mother? Was not Jacob Predestined and Esau a Reprobate? Does Christ not say in the gospel that there will be two men in a field on Judgment Day; one shall be saved and the other condemned? Is not the one who is saved Predestined; is not the one who is lost Reprobate?

Then let us consider carefully where our Predestined Brothers have traveled and where the Brothers Reprobate have journeyed. We see that, by those same respective pathways, the Reprobates came to their end in Hell and the Predestined ended up in Glory. Be enlightened, oh, you Pilgrims that read this story;

for there is no path to the Paradise of Glory other than the one taken by Pre-destined Pilgrim. Nor is there a way to Hell other than that of Pilgrim Repro-bate. Embrace disillusionment, for through the vanity of life—through exces-sive wealth; through voluptuousness, sensuality, and pleasures of the flesh; by seeking honor and revenge—one shall go directly to Babylon, which is Hell. Be enlightened, for only through becoming disillusioned with this world—through piety and devotion, through observance of the Law of God, through penance and tribulations, through the love and charity of God—can one go safely to Jerusa-lem, or Glory.

∼

FINIS

LAUS DEO,
VIRGINIQUE MATRI.

Index